Québec
Goes

If Québec Goes...

28/246 407

The

Real

Cost

of

Separation

Marcel Côté / David Johnston

Published in 1995 by
Stoddart Publishing Co. Limited
34 Lesmill Road
Toronto, Canada
M3B 2T6
Tel. (416) 445-3333
Fax (416) 445-5967

Stoddart Books are available for bulk purchase for
sales promotions, premiums, fundraising, and seminars.
For details, contact the **Special Sales Department** at
the above address.

ISBN: 0-7737-5742-2

Cover Design: Bill Douglas/The Bang
Typesetting: Tony Gordon
Printed and bound in Canada

*Stoddart Publishing gratefully acknowledges the support
of the Canada Council, the Ontario Ministry of Culture,
Tourism, and Recreation, Ontario Arts Council, and
Ontario Publishing Centre in the development of writing
and publishing in Canada.*

Contents

List of Illustrations

Preface

This is a conversation between two friends — about our city, Montréal, our province, Québec, and our country, Canada. The separation of Québec is a serious possibility, which might be decided in the Québec referendum to be held within a few months. Our book examines the cost of separation, for Québec and for Canada, but is written primarily for our fellow Québecers, because they will have to make a formal choice about the country of their future in the upcoming referendum. But it is also written for Canadians in other provinces, to explain what is at stake, and to describe the folly that has resulted from our incapacity as a country to rearrange the structure of our nation.

There is a companion book, *Le Rêve de la terre promise: les coûts de l'indépendance*, a French version authored by Marcel. Indeed, the French version is the original work upon which this book is based. The topic and conclusions are the same, but the language, in more than one way, is different. The initial book was written for a Québécois audience. Upon reading it for review, David suggested the English book and wrote a first draft.

We had first met some fifteen years ago, a few months after David moved to Montréal as principal of McGill University. The occasion was a meeting of the Montréal Chamber of Commerce to discuss McGill's role in the city. Our paths have crossed several times since then.

We both come from small mining towns. David was born in Sudbury and grew up in Sault Ste. Marie, in northern Ontario. Marcel is from Malartic in northern Québec. Both of us attended university in the United States in the 1960s. David studied at Harvard in Boston and then pursued law at Cambridge in England. Marcel was an economics student at Carnegie Mellon in Pittsburgh. We have both taught: Marcel for a few years at Université de Sherbrooke and at Université du Québec à Montréal and David at Queen's University, the University of Toronto, Western Ontario, where he was dean of law, and finally McGill. David was principal of McGill for fifteen years and is now professor of law at McGill's Centre for Medicine, Ethics, and Law.

Marcel's career has focused on economics and consulting as a strategic planner. He was one of the co-founders of Groupe Secor in 1975, which over the years has become one of Canada's most respected consulting firms and where he is presently a senior partner. Marcel is well known for his role as an economic and strategic adviser to Québec's premier, Robert Bourassa, in the mid-1980s and to the prime minister of Canada a few years later

We are both Montréalers. As befits our individual backgrounds, David would call himself both a Canadian and a Québecer, and Marcel both a Québécois and a Canadian. We are both bilingual. Marcel learned English in his youth in the mines of Malartic. David learned French upon coming to Montréal, at the age of 37.

If separation were to come, both of us would bear the consequences. Marcel would definitely stick with Montréal, despite the severe problems that would be caused by the choice of his compatriots. Would David stay? It is too early to tell. This would involve an agonizing family decision.

But we do not think it will happen. Three years ago, an economist compared the separation of Québec to white-water rafting on a tumultuous river. Today's conditions have worsened, thanks largely to the Canadian public debt crisis. A national divorce at this time would be foolish for both parties. Canadians can do better with their inheritance. Looking squarely at the cost of a divorce should make us summon the wisdom to deal effectively with longstanding problems that have been left to fester over the years.

The idea of this book rests on the assumption that we live in a liberal democracy, and that public, reasonable debate should guide collective decisions. Beyond this belief in a shared rationality, we both share a concern that the debate over Québec's and Canada's destiny at times has been cloudy and confused. This more than anything else explains the tone of our book and our decision to leave the footnotes and extensive bibliography to the original French version.

We took the time to write this book in the belief that it will influence, for the better, the evolution of our society, well beyond the upcoming vote. Hard work, a strong sense of justice, equality of opportunity, the drive for excellence — these, more than anything else, are the ingredients that make up good societies. This is what our country is all about, not power and politicians, government, or even the social safety net.

And what of our children — and theirs? Will they have taken from them the right to be Québécois-Canadian or Canadian-Québécois, the blessing of living in the fairest and most civil society in the world? That question, running through our imaginations, is what impelled us to put our conversation between these covers. We want others to have the same conversation, particularly with their children.

For the values that make this country precious are also rooted in families. We therefore dedicate this work to our own families, who are sharing this magnificent journey with us, through the good and the hard times.

MARCEL CÔTÉ, DAVID JOHNSTON
MONTRÉAL

Acknowledgements

This book, like most books, is the fruit of the cooperation of a large number of people who toiled anonymously behind the scenes. We wish to thank them all.

In 1992, John McCallum co-authored, with Marcel, an 80-page essay on the cost of separation — the seed of this book. Since then, John has been a constant adviser, especially in the writing of the original French edition of this work.

Over the years, many people have helped shape our thoughts on constitutional issues. Marcel acknowledges the contribution of Tom Courchesne, Roger Miller, Reed Scowen, Pat Grady, André Raynault, Claude Castonguay, Bryan Campbell, Tom Kierans, Daniel Latouche, and Claude Beauchamps. Special mention should also be made of the C. D. Howe Institute, which over the years has provided a significant forum to debate the issue and has published so many useful studies.

We would like to thank Paul Richard, Robert Dyotte, Clément Gignac, Madeleine Bélanger, and André Dauphinais, who have helped with research, and the numerous friends who read and commented on the early draft of the French version.

Michèle Bazin, who for the past several years has been encouraging Marcel to write this book, has read and commented on the first drafts and was instrumental in securing a French publisher.

Our editor, Donald G. Bastian, and his team at Stoddart have managed the remarkable feat of getting this book published on time under impossible deadlines. Their highly professional participation has greatly enhanced the quality of our book. Céline Boivert and Ann Brodie, our personal assistants, ensured that things were done while we were on the road and, as always, have performed miracles behind our backs.

Finally, Marcel would like to thank his colleagues at Groupe Secor, who over the years have supported him while he was participating in this great Canadian debate — an unusual arrangement that testifies to a very special partnership.

1

The Promised Land?

David Johnston: *Before we discuss the costs of separation, let me ask, why do so many Québecers want to separate from Canada?*

Marcel Côté: And let me give their response: Why shouldn't Québecers have their own country? We are a distinctive people. Most other peoples of the world have their own country. If the Danes, Norwegians, and Swedes can have their own country, flourish in their own language, and succeed economically, why shouldn't we Québecers do the same?

We now share a country with the Canadians, these separatists go on. But we are a minority. We don't control all the tools of development held by a people. Why could we not, like sensible grownups, put an end to this baleful tutelage and become good neighbours with Canada?

An independent Québec would be the same geographically as

today. But all our taxes would be paid to Québec. The Québec government alone would carry the responsibilities currently borne by the federal government, from old-age pensions to national defence.

An independent Québec — what would it be like?

They say Québec would be a country with seven million citizens ranking among the richest countries of the world. Consider Sweden, the Netherlands, and Denmark, other smaller countries where the population is under ten million. They manage well, socially and economically. We would equal France in standard of living, slightly surpass Italy, and exceed Britain by 10%.

Québec would maintain close connections with Canada, its natural partner, in these Québecers' view. There would evidently be no customs barriers between Québec and Canada. It would be just like today! We would use the Canadian dollar. In many ways, nothing would change.

Our relations with the United States would be broadly similar to today, they claim. Québec would be a party to the North American Free Trade Agreement (NAFTA) and the General Agreement on Tariffs and Trade (GATT), the club of exporting nations who define the rules of international commerce.

Québec would obviously be a member of the United Nations, they say, joining 185 other countries. We would have ambassadors in the major countries of the world. Our present Québec delegations would simply be converted into embassies; we would add another dozen new ambassadors.

We would have an army and could actually become members of NATO and NORAD, those mutual defence organizations to which

Canada belongs. We would have a foreign-aid program, thus repatriating our share of these responsibilities.

They also believe that Québec would be a more intelligent country than Canada is with Québec as part of it. We would terminate the impossible compromises required of an illogical country. Canada extends from the Pacific to the Atlantic, with ten provinces, three territories, a significant number of native peoples, and especially two "nations," each with its own language. Why should we impose our views on Albertans? Why should Albertans have a word to say on the affairs of Québecers?

And that's not the end of their optimism about Québec as an independent country. Duplication of two levels of government, federal and provincial, along with their perpetual quarrels, would end. Jurisdictions would be clear. As the New England poet Robert Frost said: "Good fences make good neighbors."

That would also allow the Québec government to decentralize. Concentration of power in Québec City in the hands of a small number of civil servants would end. As we often say here, Québec would become the "Québec of the regions." Each region within Québec would take responsibility for its own development.

Would Québec be as well off economically in their view?
In 1991 and 1992, the Bélanger-Campeau Commission invited a number of economic submissions on this question. Some asserted that Québec would lose because it would sever the Canadian economic union. The break would not be total, because intergovernmental agreements would be negotiated. But two countries remain two countries. No treaty or entente can paper over this reality.

Nevertheless, other economists emphasized that the disadvantages would not be substantial. Little countries in a common market get on quite well. Switzerland and Québec have the same population. Switzerland, not even a member of the European Union, is the world's second richest country.

Québec would be more dynamic as an independent country, the separatists say.

Jane Jacobs, a well-known specialist on economic growth who lives in Toronto, has defended this thesis in a book published in 1978, *The Question of Separation: Québec and the Struggle over Sovereignty*. There is nothing like being masters of your own destiny to stir your blood. Québecers, in an independent country, would be forced to excel. They could no longer benefit from the Canadian equalization system that helps them through difficult years. Equalization pools taxes from all regions of Canada and redistributes wealth in an egalitarian fashion through federal expenditure. Poorer regions, and areas caught in a recession, benefit. This would no longer be the case in an independent Québec.

But you are referring to selected studies only and ones done for the Bélanger-Campeau Commission. These were intended to make the best case for Québec bargaining in the pre-Charlottetown Accord era.

True. I speak of "a promised land." One of the most thorough economic studies of an independent Québec was done by the Economic Council of Canada in 1991. Well-known separatists like trade unionists Marcel Pépin and Pierre Paquette, along with staunch federalists such as Roger Phillips, Gordon Osbaldston, and Léon Courville, sat on this council. They approved the conclusions. This study examined different scenarios for Canada from the status quo to Québec separation. It concluded that an independent Québec would be penalized economically. The permanent cost was estimated at 3% of the economy, a permanent shortfall. This would result principally from the loss of the Canadian equalization system. This equals a 3% tax on everything an independent Québec produces. Jacques Parizeau, now the premier of Québec, appraised the study as a serious work based on a solid methodology.

How do separatists reply to this?

They say that even if Québec loses Canadian equalization and its 3%, independence would make this up plus more. Québec would be better administered. Federal-provincial confusion in economic management would end. Endless jurisdictional conflicts, which sap the strength of economic policies and inhibit realization of full economic potential, would fade into the night. A single level of government, a unitary system, would produce better results than the current federal system in which two levels often compete.

But evidence on that is far from clear.

Yes. The world is divided between unitary systems like France and Japan, and federal regimes like the United States, Germany, and Canada. Some specialists emphasize that federalism yields better results than unitary systems, because of beneficial competition between levels of government. The principal drawback of unitary governments is the way they bury themselves in bureaucracy. They rapidly become ineffective, paralysed by contradictory interests. On paper, a unitary government appears attractive. In practice, it is different, like a monopoly. On paper a monopoly can always show lower costs. In practice a monopoly becomes more costly due to lack of competition and consumer choice.

Can you illustrate your argument?

Yes. Education belongs exclusively to Québec. We are a unitary regime in this respect. Québecers cannot blame any other level of government for education's current state.

So how are we doing? At best, our educational system is mediocre. Many reports confirm this. For example, only one youth in two finishes secondary school (grade 11) in the Catholic School Commission of Montréal. After Alberta, Québec has the highest dropout rate at the secondary level in Canada, 30%. It is 40% in Montréal. In New Brunswick, 15%. The majority of students cannot write proper French upon graduation. We spend more than $7132 per student at the primary and secondary level, the highest in Canada and one of the world's highest, with unimpressive results.

Is the Québec government concerned?

Of course. But it exercises a monopoly. It doesn't have to worry about competition. Education, more than anything else, guarantees our future as a people. Yet during the last Québec election our politicians scarcely blinked at the subject, other than to decry the closing of primary schools in some communities.

Any other examples?

Yes, several. Managing the hospital system belongs solely to Québec. Is it well managed? You judge. Québecers surely do not think so. You should also judge skeptically the extent of decentralization promised in an independent Québec.

Another sector — construction — strikingly exposes the myth of excellent "unitary" management. For 20 years this sector has been a mess, with strikes, vandalism, destruction, restrictive practices, violence, lower productivity, and so on.

The federal government is totally absent from this sector. For 20 years the Québec government has intervened in it, without success. In 1994 a law deregulated it. In 1995 another law reregulated it. The 20-year folly continues. The promised land has no miracle in construction.

Education, the hospital system, and construction constitute good barometers to measure the probable efficiency of unitary government in an independent Québec.

But what about duplications between the national and provincial governments in the current federal system?

Take an example where the duplication is flagrant: French public television. Radio-Canada and Radio-Québec function side by side. There is a program budget of $320-million for the one and $50-million for the other. Certainly there is duplication. But are the two exactly the same? No, each chain specializes. What's more, each watches and copies the best initiatives of the other. In an independent Québec, I doubt we could do better. One could abolish one of the two chains and thus cut services. One could also merge them and create a monopoly. On paper, this is much more economical and efficient. So are education, health, and construction. On paper, but not in practice.

Would the promised land that is an independent Québec be very different from the Québec of today?

Let's answer that by examining Québec's situation in Canada now.

2

The Country We Now Have

Canada is the largest country in the world in terms of land. It is among the least densely inhabited. A very large part, in the north, is scarcely populated at all. So, too, for Québec. In land mass it represents 23% of Canada; in population, 25%.

The Canadian economy is eighth in the world by size, following six other substantially industrialized countries, and China. But Canada remains fifth in individual wealth, after the United States and Switzerland, and just behind Japan and Germany. The table below shows the purchasing power of different countries. City-states were excluded.

*

David Johnston: *What about Québec's situation in the world economy?*

Marcel Côté: Québec's Gross Domestic Product (GDP) per capita is 9% below Canada's average. In purchasing power, the gap is less than 5%. This places the average Québecer's living standard at the

Table 1
The sixteen richest countries (1993)

	GDP per capita $000	Index			GDP per capita $000	Index
1 United States	24.7	100	9	Austria	18.8	76.1
2 Switzerland	23.6	95.5	10	Belgium	18.5	74.9
3 Japan	21.1	85.4	11	Australia	18.5	74.9
4 Germany	21.0	85.0	12	Italy	18.1	73.2
5 Canada	20.4	82.5	13	Netherlands	18.1	73.2
6 France	19.4	78.5	14	United Kingdom	17.7	71.7
7 Norway	19.1	77.3	15	Sweden	17.6	71.2
8 Denmark	18.9	76.5	16	Iceland	17.2	69.6

Source: World Bank Atlas, 1995

78th index, at the same level, among the industrialized countries, as France and ahead of countries like Norway, Sweden, and Australia.

What bearing do the political systems have on the economies of these countries?

Four of the five richest are federal regimes, like Canada, with the oft-cited duplications and inefficiencies deplored by the prophets of the promised land. Germany, in fifth place, is also a federal regime. France, the epitome of unitary countries, is in sixth place. If anything, competition between levels of government promotes economic wealth.

But federal or unitary systems aside, what about Québec's economic situation?

All is not rosy for Québec. Unemployment is high. Table 2 shows it to be among the highest in the industrialized world.

Table 2
Unemployment rates, autumn 1994

1 Spain	24.3	9 United Kingdom	8.9
2 Belgium	14.3	10 Germany	8.2
3 France	12.6	11 Holland	7.6
4 Italy	11.9	12 Sweden	7.4
5 Québec	11.8	13 Austria	6.1
6 Denmark	11.7	14 United States	5.8
7 Canada without Québec	9.8	15 Switzerland	4.4
8 Australia	9.1	16 Japan	3.0

Source: The Economist Intelligence Unit

Québec doesn't head the list for unemployment. Large unitary countries like France, Italy, and Spain have worse rates of unemployment than Québec, in spite of the theoretical omnipotence of their form of government. Little European countries like Belgium and Denmark scarcely do better. By contrast, a large number of countries record lower unemployment rates than Québec's. The rate of unemployment of a region reflects deep-rooted characteristics. If one examines the regions of Canada, Québec has historically performed better than the Atlantic provinces, but much worse than Ontario and the western provinces. Interregional mobility of labour, more than any other factor, explains these regional characteristics. Independence would not change this situation. In fact, it would worsen it. Interregional mobility would decrease further.

Important regional disparities also exist within Québec. The average unemployment rate in the more distant regions, such as Saguenay-Lac St.-Jean, North Coast, Lower St. Lawrence-Gaspé, was 13% to 16%

in the autumn of 1994, contrasted with less than 12% in Montréal. The gap in revenue per capita measured between the richest (Montréal and the Outaouais) and the poorest regions (Abitibi, Gaspé, Lac St.-Jean) is only one-third. Is Québec worse off than others? No. Why? Because of the Canadian redistribution system.

Can you do this comparison for other jurisdictions?
Yes, the average revenue gap between Ontarians and Newfoundlanders is 38%. Between Québec and Ontario it is only 10%. As for the United States, Mississippi is one half the rate of Massachusetts. The situation is similar in Europe. In France, the richest region (Paris) is twice as well off as the poorest (Limousin, Poitou, Auvergne, Lower Normandy). These examples demonstrate that Québec's situation, comparatively, is favourable. All industrialized countries have these disparity problems, particularly between outlying regions and large cities.

Neither federal countries like the U.S. and Germany nor unitary countries like France and Japan have simple solutions for regional disparities. Independence would not hand Québec a magic bullet. The land that we have — Québec, as a province within Canada — is a country which strangers admire as a singular international success. International polls of French, Germans, Japanese, Americans, Belgians, and Italians all give the same response. Canada is among the most applauded and envied. In the comparative surveys that select the best cities in the world, Montréal is usually in the first level, sharing the crown with several other Canadian cities, such as Vancouver and Toronto.

You started with the Québec situation, but what about the Canadian experience as a whole?

What counts most is quality of life. In this respect, Québec in Canada does well. Criminality in the province is low. Income disparities, as high as they appear to us, are less than in Europe. The rule of law prevails. Cultural life is vibrant.

We have our problems. They are the same as most industrialized countries'. Our educational system is not functioning well. We know the reasons only too well. Our health system has cracks. But is there a better one anywhere else? An aging population strains our capacities. Governments cannot respond with more funding. But similar criticisms exist in France. One hears whispers in official circles of instituting a two-tier system to absorb galloping costs. The U.S. debate rages on universality and costs; whoever has paid hospital charges in that country accepts with equanimity the faults of our system.

Though the rate is low in comparison with other countries, criminality still is a problem here; so is juvenile delinquency. We have much to learn from European countries and Japan. And we can say that we do better than the U.S. But none of this results from Québec's constitutional situation.

Let's return to our constitutional problem then. Are we Canadians unique?

No, a very large number of countries are in the same boat. Take industrialized countries, for example. In Belgium tensions are worse. In Italy the third most important party wants to separate the north from the rest of the country. Spain supports several "Québec" situations simultaneously. Several years ago the "Scottish National" party in Scotland, the separatist party, received majority support from the population. Even in Germany the Bavarians complain of being exploited by the Germans.

So tensions are normal in countries where more than one culture or people coexist?
Yes, particularly when they are regionally concentrated. Regional politicians capitalize on these tensions. But generally common sense prevails. Moreover, in the past 70 years, no democratic country has undergone separation, nor has any highly industrialized country ever. Politicians don't bear the costs of a divorce. The taxpayers do. Ultimately this reality disciplines the politicians.

Bicultural or multicultural countries aren't bad. Switzerland shares four languages and four ethnic communities. Certain regions of the United States, little by little, are becoming bicultural regions. In fact, in the majority of these regions, significant tensions exist, but politically no one foresees a political separation.

Separatism is not a uniquely Québec phenomenon. Paradoxically, the multiplication of internal instability in many other countries makes things look more normal here.

But the threat of separation is the overriding problem in Canada today!
Not so! Separatism is not Canada's principal problem. Canada suffers from an illness that has little to do with the Parti Québécois. The national illness that makes foreign investors more nervous than Québec separation is the deficit. In Ottawa, Québec City, Toronto, Fredericton, and everywhere, our governments spend borrowed money to pay for the groceries, that is, for basic operations. They have been doing so for nearly 20 years. Politicians — federalist and separatist, liberal and conservative, péquiste and others — regularly promise to eliminate the deficit. But they seldom do.

How do we compare on this score with others?

Canadians are among the world's most indebted citizens. Our net debt per capita was, according to one calculation, $32,000 in 1994. Québecers were a little "worse," at $34,000. Our provincial government is the least disciplined of the provincial governments in Canada. It recently "lifted" that distinction from Ontario.

But what makes Canada's situation worse is our foreign borrowing. Close to 40% of Canada's public debt, federal, provincial, and local, is owed to foreigners. In that regard, Québec is slightly worse than the Canadian average. Indeed, Québecers are, per capita, the largest foreign borrowers in the world, thanks to our inability to solve our deficit, and also as a result of Hydro-Québec's high amount of borrowing abroad.

This isn't exactly an enviable situation.

That's right. One must repay these debts one day. Our politicians have not yet fully understood this, or do not care. Whatever Québec's premier, Jacques Parizeau, says, reducing the deficit is not his priority this year. Politicians are all the same: every year, they find a good reason to postpone the reduction of the deficit.

But on reflection, who is at fault? Excessive debt is a very serious problem, but should we blame the politicians?

We elect and re-elect them according to our wishes. During the last campaign in Québec in 1994, we elected the politicians who made the most promises. Let's not blame others; let's look at ourselves in the mirror. In Québec and elsewhere in Canada, we don't regard debt (the historical total owed) and deficit (the current year's gap between revenue and expenditure) as serious problems.

Collectively, Québecers and Canadians can compare themselves to overweight persons with 50 extra pounds who adore desserts! "It's not a big deal, I've got a strong constitution." "It's not my fault, it's my genes."

So where does the debt problem take us?

Space does not allow for an analysis of the regime international lenders will impose on us one of these days. This will be as interesting for our society as the diets and exercise programs doctors prescribe for excessively fat persons — ones who are totally astonished to find they have heart problems.

But let's be more specific on the independence adventure. Are you saying we are scarcely in a financial condition to embark on this voyage?

Correct. Let's stop fooling ourselves. This is no time for fairy tales.

3

Looking Through Rose-Coloured Glasses

David Johnston: *You say many in Québec perceive the promised land through rose-coloured glasses. How do they get there?*
Marcel Côté: They imagine it will be relatively easy: "At first we win the referendum. The question will be clear. The wishes of Québecers will be evident. When a majority of Québecers, and I should add, a *solid* majority of francophone Québecers, clearly express their wish for an independent country, which would assume full sovereign powers, everybody should fall in line and go along with us. After all, the democratic will is powerful and convincing."

The government of Québec, according to this scenario, would then formally notify Ottawa of the democratic wish of Québecers, and will simply open negotiations so that separation can take place in an orderly way. Both parties will want Québec and Canada to profit from their good-neighbour relationship, a common political culture, 200 years of shared history, and mutually beneficial interests.

How do they see negotiations being conducted?

They may take from six to nine months, according to this scenario. "The problems are complex. But we understand these dossiers. We are a federal country. Québec and Ottawa have negotiated for 125 years. Public servants speak daily. Most senior civil servants are well acquainted with one another. Moreover, some federal public servants want to join us. We have the same accounting system."

So much for negotiations. What about the outcomes?

"The principal points of discussion are well known," they say. "For instance, what percentage of the federal debt will we inherit? How will it be transferred? The Bélanger-Campeau Commission studied this. The consensus then was clear. There may be matters for compromise. That's normal in negotiations.

"Several joint management organizations will be created. For the testing and control of new drugs, for example. The present agricultural product marketing boards, for milk and poultry, for example, should remain as joint agencies, administered by a single organization. They will all be located in Ottawa and Hull; the latter city will inherit a quarter of these organizations. More than a quarter of the public servants in these organizations will be Québécois. Their leaders will be jointly appointed. The St. Lawrence Seaway Authority, which will be administered jointly, will be the exception. Its head office will remain in Montréal.

"Most likely, and unfortunately for Québec, the Bank of Canada will not be one of these jointly administered organizations. Opposition exists in certain Canadian quarters. Québec will use the Canadian dollar. But we won't have an official voice on the board of governors of the Bank. Canadians are a little emotional on this subject. But we shall have close consultations on monetary policy. After all, a central bank cannot neglect 25% of its clientele.

"The Québec public service will absorb federal civil servants working in Québec. We will harmonize collective agreements. We will find jobs locally for federal civil servants of the Outaouais region. Some Québec ministries will be established there. Others will work for the jointly managed organizations. Finally, we will relocate to Hull certain agencies now actually situated in Québec City — the Québec automobile insurance agency, for example. We intend to create 18,000 jobs there within two years.

"These administrative transfers and the integration of civil servants will take place within one year of the proclamation of independence. And the proclamation will be set for one year following the referendum. Transfers will take place generally by ministry, although certain programs will have their own smooth rhythm of transfer. For example, in month one the federal government will issue pension cheques. In month two Québec will issue the same cheques. As a program is transferred, Québec will assume the costs. The transfer of taxes could be effective January 1 of the second year."

What about the national debt? What do they say about that?
"The Québec part of the federal debt could be transferred in two years," they say. "Québec could assume, say, 20% of this debt — $100-billion, slightly higher than the Bélanger-Campeau estimate. Québec will issue, in two years, $100-billion of additional debt, to refinance the inherited Canadian debt. Current holders of this Canadian debt will be the principal buyers of this replacement debt.

"Several administrative agreements will define the relationships between Québec and Canada. There will be an agreement on customs and immigration. This ensures there will be no border posts between Québec and Ontario. We will drive over the border without realizing that we have crossed into another country, just like we do now with provincial borders. There will be an agreement to ensure the free movement of workers and to regulate other common interests. For example, Newfoundland would be able to sell its electricity to the Maritime provinces and into the United States, thanks to a special tariff with Hydro-Québec, which controls the cross-Québec transmission lines."

Isn't this a naive set of expectations?

Separatist leaders say that their separation scenario rests on pragmatism. "Québec has a number of levers with which to negotiate. Defence is one. Canada has a strong interest in Québec participating jointly in continental defence. We would integrate a part of the Canadian armed forces, for instance by taking over the Canadian bases of Valcartier, St. Hubert, and Longue Pointe. We should conclude unified command accords, as France has already done with Germany, and Canada with the United States in NORAD.

"Even before holding the referendum, we would also conclude agreements with native peoples, recognizing their rights," they say. "Aboriginals will have significantly greater rights to autonomy in an independent Québec."

In this scenario the jurisdictional transfer is done in peace and social harmony.

Yes. "Undoubtedly there will be those who want to remain in Canada and leave Québec. Canada could allow a five-year period of grace for this. This will reassure even Montréal anglophones who are more nervous and emotional than francophone Québecers on this issue. There might even be a relaxation of several constraints in bill 101, which protects the French language. An officially French country with full power to protect its language has less need to manifest its might."

Are there not additional costs in this rosy scene?

"Access to independence will not happen without some additional costs," they say. "Jurisdictional transfers impose costs. But there are also economies that can be achieved. We will eliminate duplications, saving more than $3-billion. We will gain also by sweeping away some outdated agencies. We will probably postpone certain maintenance projects. Finally, thanks to rationalization of decision-making and elimination of duplication, the economy will perform better. No significant tax increases, no cuts in essential programs, are anticipated.

"Finally, Québec will sign international treaties, such as the free trade agreement. This benefits all the signatories. It's the same thing for GATT. Québec will open embassies in the principal countries with which it trades. And these countries will open embassies in Québec City. This will have a significant economic impact on the economy of that region.

"Independence will not cost Québecers a penny. We've repeated this often and we maintain it. There will be certain expenses. But these will be neutralized by rationalizations and elimination of duplication. This transition will be harmonious and orderly. Canadians are pragmatic. Rapid agreement meets their best interests. Business hates uncertainty. Business people will press for everyone to sit down at the table. In these negotiations, Québec, like Canada, has some important cards to play. It will be a negotiation of equals. Everything should be tied up in one year. One more year will complete the administrative transfers, two years for the debt question. There we are! The Québec people will at last become a normal people in a normal country."

Now, take off the glasses. Where are the errors in this scenario?
Nearly everywhere. The scene described is a mirage. The changes necessary for independence are of such a magnitude that they could not be done in two years, or even four. It is far from certain that negotiations with Canada, in advance of any actual changes, would succeed. Even before they begin, several months will elapse, perhaps even years. Canada is neither disposed to negotiate, nor ready to deal. Québec says let's go. It claims to have completed its analyses. But Canada has not even begun its studies. It even lacks the legal mechanisms that would allow the federal government to negotiate.

But to this the separatist leaders reply: Then we will declare independence unilaterally.
Yes, they say if the accord is not concluded one year to the day after the referendum, Québec will unilaterally proclaim its independence. "Québec cannot be held hostage. It will become independent, with or without negotiations!"

How realistic is this?
Let's answer this indirectly, with some examples. Consider the pen-

sion cheque of Mrs. Tremblay, a 75-year-old widow. She needs this money to pay her rent. Who in Québec has the file on her the day after unilateral secession? And the unemployment insurance cheque of Paul Laverdure, father of three? What happens to the job of Marie Boisvert, who works in the privy council office in Ottawa and lives in Hull? And the milk from the farm of Ludger Bourassa which, after being processed, is sold in Ontario as part of the Canadian supply management system? And the Crees of James Bay, who have not said yes? And how will the Québec minister of finance continue to borrow $5-billion per year — an average of $600-million per month — the majority of it from outside Québec? And the tax files of four million taxpayers lodged in Ottawa? And the agreements we must sign to make the transition without any discomfort?

To declare our independence unilaterally is politically unrealistic. At the moment, the people of Québec really do not understand what is involved. If they did know, they would not allow such nonsense to be presented as a realistic option.

Besides this rose-coloured scenario, let's also put aside this macho manifesto of unilateral independence. Let's examine more closely another scenario, more likely if the "yes" forces carry the day in the referendum.

All right, let us say Québec is ready to negotiate, but who on the Canadian side can negotiate with Québec?
Let's answer that by casting our minds ahead hypothetically.

4

It Takes Two to Tango

Monday, October 16, 1995, 8:42 p.m.: Pamela Wallin announces on CBC-TV that the Yes side has won the referendum. The question was clear: "Do you want Québec to become a sovereign country, a country distinct from Canada?" According to the CBC projections, with most of the polls in, 54% of Québecers have said yes. In the streets of Montréal and Québec, the indépendantistes begin their celebration. Calm returns only in the wee small hours of the night.

A scenario fictitious and improbable. But let us continue.

The next day, Tuesday, October 17, 1995, Québecers are nervous. The celebration is over. Jacques Parizeau addresses the people of Québec from the Red Room of the National Assembly at 2 p.m. As he mentioned during the campaign, the government will give Canada a full year to negotiate jurisdictional transfers and administrative arrangements; this deadline will ensure that the transition proceeds without disruption.

The prime minister of Canada addresses the nation at 7 the same evening. He reviews the referendum results. He issues an appeal for calm. He observes that Québecers have voted without truly understanding the project for an independent country. The outcome could only be determined after negotiations with the rest of Canada. He will convoke in Ottawa, on Thursday, the first ministers of the nine other provinces and the chiefs of the three territories and the three aboriginal groups.

The meeting lasts that entire Thursday. At 9:45 p.m. the prime minister again addresses the Canadian nation, speaking in French and English. A press conference follows. The first ministers, territorial leaders, and aboriginal leaders have agreed to meet again in Ottawa in two weeks, beginning November 2. In the meantime, the government leaders will hold consultations with their colleagues. Mr. Chrétien will meet Mr. Parizeau on the following Sunday, October 22, in Montréal.

But no decision has been taken at the meeting on negotiations with the Québec government. The *possibility* of a Canadian referendum has been raised. As for the native peoples, they have decided to hold referenda in Québec for each Indian and Inuit group.

But on Friday, in the House of Commons, just four days after the vote to separate, Preston Manning warns the prime minister not to hold any negotiations with Mr. Parizeau at the Montréal meeting. Newfoundland's premier, Clyde Wells, emphasizes that no negotiations should take place with Québec before Canada has decided on its own constitution. That could take several months. There is no way Newfoundland could accept an agreement that would physically isolate it from central Canada.

*

David Johnston: *So does this mean there is no mandate to negotiate?*

Marcel Côté: Let's continue the hypothetical scene. At the end of the meeting with Mr. Parizeau, Mr. Chrétien announces that the federal government cannot negotiate with the Québec government because it lacks both mandate and constitutional authority. Parizeau launches a solemn appeal to English Canada "to get its act together." Québec has clearly expressed, democratically, its wish to separate.

The meeting of first ministers and aboriginal leaders lasts for two days at the beginning of November. A coalition of premiers from the west and Atlantic provinces opposes all discussions with Québec before English Canada has determined its own future constitution without Québec. Preston Manning supports this position: "We cannot step blindfolded into a new constitutional structure," he declares. "The withdrawal of Québec equals a veto right to Ontario, which will control the House of Commons. That is unacceptable." The next day, the premier of Alberta declares that Alberta shares Preston Manning's concern about Ontario's weight in the new Canada.

On November 22 Chrétien declares that an election will take place on January 15, 1996. All the federal parties agree not to negotiate aboriginal territories with Québec without their representatives being present at the negotiations and without their agreement on any accord touching their status.

So we cast our minds ahead further to a federal election and it is now 1996?

Yes. The Liberals win 95 of 265 seats, 22 from Québec. Jean Charest's Conservatives, who urged national reconciliation, obtain 45 seats, 13

from Québec. The Bloc Québécois, which hesitated before participating in the election, obtains only 38% of the popular vote in Québec.
It elects 40 members of parliament. The Reform party wins 82 seats,
with 18 from the Maritimes. It forms the official opposition. The NDP
elects only three MPs.

The House of Commons will reconvene on February 29, 1996.
Chrétien seeks the support of the Progressive Conservatives and the
NDP to form a coalition government. The Québec file remains immo-
bile. There has not been a meeting with Mr. Parizeau since October
20 the previous year. On February 18, Parizeau sends a shot across
the bow of English Canada: "Negotiate or Québec will act unilaterally." Four days later Chrétien is again chosen prime minister of Canada
by a majority vote in the House of Commons, heading a coalition
government. One-quarter of the ministers come from Québec. Charest
is deputy prime minister and responsible for constitutional affairs.
The price for his support? A constitutional conference plus a cross-
Canada referendum devoted to recognition of the French-Canadian
people and decentralization of Canadian federalism.

What a mess! But this is only one of several possible scenarios.
We could imagine other ones more or less complicated. The Bloc
Québécois could have won the elections in Québec. Defeated in the
election, Chrétien might have resigned. The Canadian referendum
might have been held in advance. But all these scenarios on post-
referendum Canada will have points in common.

Can you summarize them?
(1) Jean Chrétien, MP, St. Maurice, will be the prime minister of Canada.
His government will not have a mandate to negotiate with Québec.

Quite possibly, there will be no negotiations to restructure Canada, or between Canada and Québec, until Chrétien has been replaced as prime minister. Such a political change would take at least six months.

(2) It will be political suicide for an English-Canadian politician to negotiate with Québec lacking a mandate reflecting a Canadian consensus. This will require a constitutional convention of all the provinces and territories and in all probability a referendum. As soon as the decision to negotiate with Québec is taken, the Canadian politicians will have nothing more to gain from a coalition with Québec or electoral support from Québec. Their priorities will be directed towards Canadian needs.

(3) English Canada will think of its own problems first and, in particular, what happens if Québec withdraws from the Canadian federal system. Provinces like Newfoundland, British Columbia, and Alberta will be much more preoccupied with the new distribution of powers in Canada without Québec than with the negotiations with Québec, with whom they will retain only a marginal relationship. They will want to resolve the first problem before tackling the second. Negotiations with Québec will pass to second-level priority after negotiations between the provinces and the future Canada.

(4) The Canadian political establishment, largely supported by international public opinion, will engage in defending the interests of the native peoples and their rights to self-government, if Québec ever separates. In fact, the native peoples of Québec will be treated in law on the same footing as the government of Québec. This will scarcely please that government and its legal advisers. To do otherwise would be, outside of Québec, "politically incorrect" to the point of suicide.

In summary, then, a victory of the Yes forces in the referendum will not make Canada any more governable constitutionally than it is today?

Less so. The negotiated withdrawal of Québec implies Canadian constitutional modifications to be agreed on by all the other nine provinces. These are dependent on provincial unanimity. That has never yet been achieved. Remember Ottawa in 1982 and Meech in 1989? Unanimity only occurred with the Charlottetown spaghetti accord of 1993 and that was rejected by referendum. Even the original constitutional accord of 1867 did not obtain unanimity; Prince Edward Island withheld its support.

So we have reached spring 1996 and still no Québec-Canada negotiations?

Right. Post-referendum negotiations would have several bridges to cross. First it would be necessary to replace Jean Chrétien. Secondly, the provinces and the federal government would have to agree on the Canada of the future, without Québec. The challenges are numerous with each province having a right of veto. With 50% of the population, Ontario's place in federal institutions will be the subject of long negotiations. The maintenance of support from rich to poor provinces will also be vexing.

The third step would be the mandate to negotiate with Québec. What will be the minimum requirements of English Canada for a total entente with Québec? One overriding principle would emerge: Québec as an independent state could not obtain more powers in the common institutions than it actually had as a province and than the provinces in the new Canada will have. The provinces will not allow a separate Québec to possess powers that it did not have as part of Canada. One can also say goodbye to any participation by Québec in the management of the Bank of Canada. In its relations with the federal government, Québec would not be better treated than the nine other provinces.

Would the provinces impose any particular constraints on the mandate to negotiate in exchange for their veto right?

There could be several. The Atlantic provinces could be very exacting. For example, Newfoundland could easily require a revision of the Churchill Falls electricity contract to transport its electricity across Québec. Such demands would be very popular in Newfoundland. A premier as "heady" as Clyde Wells could require this in return for his approval of the mandate to negotiate. Mr. Wells proved in the Meech negotiations that he is not afraid to risk everything to impose his own agenda.

Any other constraints?

The native peoples would insert their own concerns in Canada's mandate to negotiate. They would demand that the sovereignty of Québec not be recognized on aboriginal territory, including the entire north of Québec.

The mandate to negotiate resulting from this cacophony of constraints could scarcely constitute a basis of discussions acceptable to Québec. But one can see in this scenario the simple results of the Canadian political game. We know this skirmishing only too well. This doesn't change because someone wants to separate. That this results in conditions that are unacceptable to Québec is not surprising. That is the history of constitutional negotiations. It's the reason nothing has been finalized.

So how long does this Mexican stand-off last?
Possibly for several years. And then the mandate of the Parti Québécois government ends.

Could that party wait so long after a referendum victory?
The temptation for Québec to take unilateral action would be strong and become stronger. But I believe the temptation would be resisted. A unilateral declaration of independence is an abrupt divorce. Without an agreement with Canada, it carries some very high costs. The government understands this. In fact, the experience of countries which have recently separated is instructive.

Let's look at those experiences.

5

Countries That Have Crossed the Desert

Québec separatists often cite the example of countries which have become independent by peaceful methods of separation. The examples are few. The majority involve the recent disintegration of the Communist bloc or the dismantling of the great Austrian and Turkish empires at the beginning of the century.

*

David Johnston: *Do they truly apply to Québec? Do we wish to live through similar experiences in Québec?*
Marcel Côté: These two questions are pertinent. The picture looks seductive from a distance.

Let's look first at the two first separations of this century, Norway in 1902 and Ireland in 1921.
The first important point is that these were preindustrial societies. Norway occupies the west coast of the Scandinavian peninsula. In

the nineteenth century it was made a subject of its neighbour, Sweden. By 1902, Norway and Sweden had nearly the same population, about two million inhabitants each. Norway had its own parliament, but was under the Swedish crown. During a severe economic crisis, the Norwegian parliament declared its independence. Preoccupied with its own economic problems, Sweden did nothing. Thus Norway peacefully became an independent country, and its economy flourished afterwards.

Is this not pertinent for Québec?

No. In 1902 Norway was a preindustrialized country, inhabited principally by fishermen and farmers. The economy was underdeveloped. Commercial relations with Sweden were weak, compared with those linking modern countries. Government was scarcely present in the economy. Neither income taxes nor widespread public social services existed. The country resembled a collection of fishing and farming villages more than a modern state. Nothing unusual in this: this was true of all preindustrial countries. There was no debt to divide, no taxes to take back, no public service to separate, no free trade agreement to renegotiate. Save for a tiny business elite, no one had mortgages or bank accounts. It was a little like Canadian confederation in 1867. In the Québec villages at that time very few people noticed any change. What counted in this epoch of the preindustrial economy was the weather for the harvest. But Québec in 1995 lives in another world.

Ireland's separation was in 1921. That country was more aligned economically with Britain.

It was Norway repeated but with some nuances. Ireland was a poorer country than Norway. Britain provided even fewer governmental services than Sweden offered Norway. The economy was also agricultural. Independence was obtained by force, following violent clashes that lasted several years. The Irish economy, very poor before independence, continued to be so after: independence changed nothing. But as Québécois indépendantistes are wont to remark, Ireland continued to use British currency for nearly ten years after its independence period.

Is this not a relevant example? Québec wants to use the Canadian dollar after independence.
It's a bad example. In 1921 in Ireland the average citizen did not have a bank account and had never written a cheque in his life. For money all he used were metal coins and sometimes bank notes. There was a financial economy in Ireland, but it was limited to several thousand people, mainly merchants and land owners in Dublin. The government borrowed little. People did not have accumulated savings. Such an economy, meagre and with an underdeveloped financial sector, could keep using British currency for a certain period of time.

And in Québec today it is dramatically different?
Yes, dramatically. There is a highly developed, sophisticated financial sector. The assets of our two principal private financial institutions, the Banque Nationale and Le Mouvement Desjardins, equal the gross national product. In Ireland, there were no such sectors. Today even countries with the most primitive economies are more developed than Ireland of 1921 and have their own currencies. The Maastricht

Treaty articulated certain conditions for a country to share a common currency. Québec is very far from meeting those conditions.

Let's examine separations after World War I.
Some years after the Irish revolution, Finland profited from the Russian Revolution to separate from Russia, following a popular uprising and some armed engagements. Russia was the historic oppressor of Finland, but it was engaged in civil war. This permitted Finland to succeed in its uprising. Separation was nevertheless effected in misery. The costs were high. But they were not different from the costs stemming from the Russian Revolution and from the just-ended Great War. Of all twentieth-century separations, Finland's nevertheless was probably the least difficult, because it happened during a full economic crisis and while a tide of troubles raged across Russia.

Are there other instructive examples of separation prior to the recent breakup of the Soviet Union?
None of significance for our discussion. One should exclude some dissolutions of artificial countries following decolonization in Africa and Asia, and notably India and Pakistan and the expulsion of Singapore from the Malaysian Federation. Mr. Parizeau publicly hailed the 1989 declaration of independence of three little Baltic republics, Estonia, Lithuania, and Latvia, when they democratically left their forced union with Russia.

Is the experience of these three republics instructive?
These were probably the countries of the former Soviet Union for which separation was the least painful. Yet it was still quite costly.

What Mr. Parizeau does not explain is the very large economic crisis which followed this dislocation. Unemployment shot up to more than 15%. Economic production fell backwards for several years, by about 30%. Inflation exploded. The new Baltic currencies lost much of their value. People who were strangers to poverty were obliged to beg. Older people, who had been living on their pensions, were particularly hard-struck. The crisis was so serious that two of the three republics returned the former Communists to power. They rejected the politicians who brought freedom from tyranny.

But who was at fault? Was it independence or the transition from communism to capitalism?
Probably both. To mix the two at the same time does not help things. Never again can a Québec politician cite favourably the Baltic countries to demonstrate that independence can occur painlessly. Economically, these separations were gruesome.

Tensions with Russia didn't help. The Baltic countries contained important Russian minorities who were against separation. Independence was unilaterally declared. The Russians replied with selective embargoes. The Baltics were significant suppliers to Russia. Commerce was severely disrupted.

Divorces are rarely happy events. The Baltic countries tasted Russian bitterness.

The example which is most current is Slovakia.
Yes, the one which Mr. Parizeau seldom quotes. The Slovak politicians "created" independence, without a referendum, in the space of some months, in 1993. Czechoslovakia had been formed in 1920. It

was a federation of two republics, the Czech and the Slovak. After the overthrow of the Soviets in the "velvet revolution" in 1988, separatist politicians were elected in 1993 to head the government of Slovakia. Negotiations were launched between the two "provinces" to dismember the federal government and sever the two republics, transforming them into two independent countries. Slovakia did not submit the question to a referendum, for fear it would be defeated.

Negotiations began in the summer of 1993. Separation took place on the following January 1. The central government was dismembered. Some ententes for common institutions replaced it. But the common currency, object of one of these ententes, lasted scarcely five weeks, as many observers had predicted. Following a liquidity crisis, Slovakia was forced to issue its own currency.

Mr. Parizeau apart, one does not hear much of Slovakia in Québec. Just how relevant is it to our discussion?
Let's examine first the less pertinent aspects. The negotiations took place one on one, between two subordinate governments who had convened to dismember the federal government. All this happened rapidly. Canada would be quite different. Negotiations would involve more than ten players. For the English, it is not a question of dismembering the federal government. English Canada would rather reorganize Canada, parallel with negotiations with Québec. Rather than one government on the other side of the table, there would be ten, or thirteen, or sixteen, depending on the role accorded to the territories and the aboriginals. As Canadian constitutional experience has demonstrated so well, such negotiations are not easy. Québec will have absolutely nothing to say on what happens on the other side of the

table with the Canadian parties negotiating between themselves.

The Slovakian separation occurred rapidly because it was not democratic. There was no referendum, neither on the mandate nor on the final accord. Had there been a referendum, separation likely would have been defeated. Absent democracy, things are simpler. But Québec *is* democratic.

But at least the separation of Slovakia was "trouble free"?

Yes, some characterize it as "the velvet divorce." However, all was not soft and smooth in this split, though there were no armed clashes. In fact, there was much bitterness in the air. The Czechs did not emerge perfectly. But making the best of it, they simply turned their backs on Slovakia. They said, "Good riddance! You wanted to separate: then separate." Moreover, the Czechs were hardnosed during the negotiations. They refused numerous economic association measures proposed by the Slovak separatists. Each took its chips and left the table. Common agreements were of minimal importance. The Slovaks were surprised. They found themselves alone in their corner. Good commercial relations with the Czechs turned sour. Slovaks discovered much more difficulty working in the Czech Republic. They suddenly became strangers in their old home. Even a "velvet" divorce is unpleasant. It leaves an acidic aftertaste.

What is the key lesson to draw here for Québec?

Some separatist leaders cast the separation of Québec as a new marriage with Canada. This characterization is not sustainable. If the experience of others is our guide, separation will be a divorce, with much bitterness. Politically, the Canadian negotiators will have their hands tied. They will be unable to make many concessions to Québec, or negotiate many collaborative ententes. The rules of divorce would be simple: each will take its assets and leave the house. Two new countries would turn their backs on one another. If Czechoslovakia is a relevant example of separation done with little pain, Canada would take its chips, turn around, and for lack of better words, say: "Good riddance." And Québec should forget about all these smooth bilateral agreements. Canada will not be in a warm mood to negotiate an agreement.

What was the economic cost of this Czech-Slovak separation which supposedly took place painlessly?

It is difficult to quantify because a second important change was also occurring. Three years earlier the two countries had begun their conversion from communism to capitalism. The effect of this transition cannot be isolated from separation. Yet the catastrophe economists predicted for Slovakia happened, in part because it was so unprepared for a capitalist economy. The Czechs were much better suited to slough off communism for a market economy. The Czech Republic is probably the East European country now functioning the best of all the countries of the former Soviet bloc.

What happened to Slovakia after separation?

Economic production fell. It dropped 9% in two years. In the Czech Republic it increased by 2%. Unemployment climbed by 3%; inflation totalled 40% in two years; pensioners were reduced to ruin. What would not "happen," in the words of the separatists, happened. It is hardly surprising that, in the last elections, the Slovakian voters opted to stop the change. But the die was cast. They could not blame communism anymore. Separation, and its consequences, caused their misfortune. The promised land was not what the Slovakian politicians had promised.

Meanwhile, the Czech Republic thrived. Free from the burden of the Slovak Republic, the Czech's accelerated the transition of their economy. Furthermore, because their economy was twice as big as Slovakia's, it was less damaged by the severing of links. In 1995, economic growth will be more than 3%. The Czech economy was more suited to a transition to a capitalist economy. The Slovak economy was more dependent on the Czech for its health than the Slovak leaders understood.

But can one not argue that what happened to Slovakia was only temporary economic transition costs?

Hardly. What caused Slovakia to stagger even deeper into economic confusion were four blows: First, their transfer payments from the central government ceased. In all federations, the poorer regions receive transfer payments. Being less well off, their taxpayers pay less to the federal government, although they receive the same level of services. The second blow was the loss of markets, particularly in the Czech Republic. The Czechs supported their own. They left the Slovaks to cope alone. The third blow? Currency. Following a liquidity crisis, the Slovakian government was forced to print its own currency. It quickly lost its value. The entire Slovak economy suffered. The fourth blow? Investors abandoned Slovakia. The country was in crisis. It offered few business opportunities.

Will Slovakia eventually recover?

It will survive economically. It has seriously fallen behind the Czech Republic; it will be poorer than before.

Is this relevant for Québec?

Yes and no. Yes, in the sense that one must not believe politicians who say that independence is painless. Yes, when one prophesies a new country can simply piggyback on another country's currency and does not think it through. Piggyback currencies did not work in Slovakia. They have not worked in modern industrialized economies.

But the answer is no in the sense that Slovakia was a poor country. It had a scarcely developed market economy. The typical Québec family has assets, property, house, bank account, retirement savings account, and also debts, mortgage, and credit cards. Our average revenue is seven to eight times that of Slovakia; the wealth of an average family, fifteen to twenty times. We have much greater means. And we have much more at risk.

No, Slovakia is not a relevant example because separation was not done democratically. There was no referendum, neither before nor after separation. The economy was also already in crisis, more seriously than anything we have ever known in Québec. Of greatest importance, the level of development of Slovakia is a fraction of ours. In fact, there has never been a case of separation involving an economy as developed as ours.

So Québec is unique in this experiment?

Let me answer your question with some questions of my own. Are Québecers ready to undertake this voyage into uncharted seas and rupture links with Canada? Are we strong enough economically to suffer a temporary but significant reduction in our standard of living? Do we accept the perturbations that will follow if the transfers of responsibilities between governments do not occur as anticipated? Are we ready to accept the strong probability that within several months of independence, the Québec government, hit by a severe liquidity crisis, will issue a Québec distress dollar to replace the Canadian dollar? In Slovakia and in the ex-republics of the Soviet Union, the population was accustomed to corrupt and ineffective governments. We are used to better public governments. Will Québecers tolerate errors of this magnitude?

6

The Desert Crossing

David Johnston: *You have stressed that the negotiations for separation will be difficult and tortuous, but what about separation itself?*

Marcel Côté: The separation of Québec, if it ever occurs, would not take place in four simple movements like a Haydn symphony. There would not be any beautiful music at all.

The discussions would be long, sown with contradictions, hesitations, stalling, and crisis. Divorces of countries are much more difficult than with people. There are no presiding judges. The two parties must agree, or slam the door, without an accord. This could happen if the government of Québec, frustrated by fruitless negotiations, unilaterally declared independence. The two parties would be bitter, whether there was an agreement or not.

Let us examine this desert passage that Québecers would have

to undertake to attain the promised land of an independent Québec.

A perilous journey is inevitable. The Slovaks experienced it. So did the Baltics. All countries that separate must go through a period of transition and adjustments. Québec would not escape.

But what about the actual adjustments that Québec would have to make?

First let's look at the global picture. There would be four types of adjustments, as indicated in Figure 1. We will visit each in more detail. Even if each of these adjustments was not critical in itself, their combination is explosive. Concurrence of events would make the desert passage extremely difficult, if not politically impossible.

But for the moment, spell them out in sequence and in order of priority.

First would be changes in basic economic conditions. Economists would call these the "real" shocks following separation. The term "real" signifies that the shocks affect the organization of the economy and not finances or taxes. Note that the *entire* economy of Québec would not be affected by these shocks. Some large economic sectors would escape largely unscathed. Trees would continue growing and pulp and paper mills would forward their fibre across the world. Aluminum refineries would transform power and bauxite into ingots. But other important sectors of the economy would be profoundly touched, precipitating a recession. Envision these "real" shocks as torpedoes cutting through defences in the economy. They carry in their wake great damage. Just as three or four torpedoes can sink a

Figure 1
Convergence of adjustment pressures

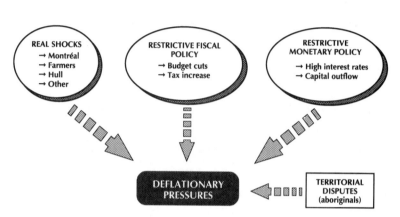

battleship while simply opening some holes in its armoured sides, these four real shocks would drop an economy into a recession.

What is the first torpedo, the one that would do the most damage?
The one striking the Montréal economy. It would be devastating. And it has to do with the reaction of anglophone Québecers to separation. Nearly 30% of Montréal's population is anglophone. Thousands of businesses and head offices in the region are controlled by anglophones. These Montréalers live in English. They want to continue to live in English. Most will not live in a country where they will be a linguistic minority. Hundreds of thousands of Montréal anglophones would leave an independent Québec. This is a normal phenomenon. Whenever a country separates, enormous emigration ensues among the newly created minorities.

So what would the first economic implications be?

Most sectors would be hit. For instance, the construction industry in Montréal would limp along for several years, trying to absorb the loss of population and activity. Business service activities downtown would be hit by head-office downscaling.

And the second torpedo?

This would strike the producers of processed milk, one-quarter of the Québec agricultural economy. It would cut their market by half in a few weeks.

And the third?

This would explode the economy of the Hull-Gatineau region, with two aftershocks: loss of federal government jobs, the base of that economy, and restrictions on working in Ontario. This explosion would reduce the richest region in Québec to the poorest within a few years.

The final torpedo?

The Canadian economic market would become a foreign market, regulated by another government. To sell in Canada or to go to work in Canada would be much more difficult than today. Numerous existing arrangements which ease trade would be discontinued.

The American market offers the best example to picture this change. It is much more complicated to sell or work in the United States than in other provinces. Canada and Québec would be two different countries. Whether they were friends or not, and whether or not a free trade agreement was struck, this reality would not change.

There would also be border posts, with verification of identities and goods. These exist between all countries, even friendly ones. One would need a permit to work in Canada. Except in exceptional circumstances, a Québec citizen would no longer work for the Canadian government. Canada-wide market agreements would cease to exist, at least in their present form. Each country would take care of its own. For a Québecer to sue an enterprise in Ontario would require procedures before the courts of a foreign country, and probably a place of business there. A Canadian regulatory tribunal would no longer oversee the telephone tariffs of Bell Canada in Québec. That company would be divided into two companies, with the Québec one relegated to the level of a subsidiary.

Let's look at the second major adjustment.

This has to do with government fiscal policy and repatriation of taxes from Ottawa and, simultaneously, the taking of responsibility for expenditures. With this there would be expenditure cuts.

The péquistes want to limit the cuts to elimination of duplication and waste. But much deeper cuts are required to meet the transition costs of independence. Tax hikes are also likely.

Fiscal policy would be paradoxical. The Québec government, seized with a full economic crisis from the "real" shock, would have to pursue a restrictive fiscal policy. It would withdraw money from the economy. It would have to meet international lenders' requirements. All these effects would be concentrated in Québec. The multiplier effects of governmental spending would work in reverse. That is, for each dollar withdrawn from the economy, another dollar's worth of economic activity would be suspended as an indirect consequence or ripple effect. The inevitability of this restrictive fiscal policy is predictable. The government has chosen independence — an exercise difficult in itself — while the combined finances of the federal and provincial governments are in very bad shape. International financial markets would obligate the Québec government to put order into its finances at the same time as it became independent.

And the third adjustment?

We call this monetary. It would be caused mostly by you and me, your mother and mine, and many other people. What do you do when a huge storm catches you when you are in the middle of the field without protection? You cover your head and rapidly run to the nearest tree. Consider what a large percentage of seven million Québecers would do when things began to sour and governments bickered. They would cover their heads and try to find shelter as promptly as possible. They would avoid being hostage to quarrelling governments. In practical terms, many — your mother and mine — would call their bank manager to say, "Shelter my money until the storm is over."

Money would make itself scarce. Savers — particularly big savers — would not take risks. They control a large part of the country's savings and suddenly would feel very fearful. Flights of capital from banks, credit unions, and brokerage houses in Québec would follow: nothing dramatic taken individually, just money put under shelter during the storm. But the combined effect of these thousands of individual acts and the reaction of the banks would be critical. The banks would have to replenish their "float" with other money, or reduce their loans. In crises, the banking system has liquidity problems — always.

In concrete terms, monetary policy would turn very restrictive, notwithstanding the wishes of the Québec government. Mr. Parizeau wants to use the Canadian dollar in a sovereign Québec. So far so good. But the Bank of Canada would say to the banks who use the Canadian dollar in Québec, "Balance your books. Replace the money which leaves Québec with fresh deposits or cut your loans." Québec would not start off on a good foot. Collectively, we borrow from abroad — even more than the rest of Canada does. We would have to borrow even more to replace the money that would leave Québec. Lacking borrowing power, we would have to cut. Then, like lightning, a true liquidity crisis would strike. Nothing surprising here; such crises are "normal" when countries separate. But the timing would be terrible.

And the last adjustment?

This has to do with the aboriginal peoples and territorial quarrels. As if one needed this. It would be the Indians, especially, who would "make trouble." The equation is simple: They don't want our independence; they have other priorities. They also have well-placed friends almost everywhere in the world. So they will make trouble.

Have you understood the enormity of what I've said? Québecers think that Indians who refuse to accept the democratic verdict of Québec and want to separate their territory from Québec are just "making trouble."

But haven't we lived with this "trouble" for fifteen or twenty years?

Yes. But now there's a new element. Who would cause the real problem? For 99% of the entire world not the Indians, but we Québecers! The Indians don't want to change anything: they want the status quo.

Québecers want to change their country. So yesterday you were Canadians. So today you are Québecers! Like hockey players who are traded!

Seen from a Québecer's perspective, Québec extends from the American border up to Ungava Bay. Seen from the Cree Indian perspective, their territory runs from the Whapmagoostui River (what the European colonists called Grande Baleine or Great Whale) up to Lake Mistassini. The Inuit country is higher up; that of the Algonquins a little lower. As long as no one got upset by the appellation "country," there was no problem. But now we Québecers dare to say that's our country right up to the top, right across Indian and Inuit "country." Now there's a problem!

So it is we who "make trouble"?

Yes, it is we who cause this big problem. We would be the bad guys worldwide. Sure, there would be hypocrites. Many Canadians would suddenly "discover" an affinity with the aspirations of the Indians of Québec. But there would be more than hypocrites supporting the Indians. French, Swedes, Japanese, Americans, Mexicans, indeed, almost everyone would support them. If the problem had taken place in Mexico, we Québecers would also support the Indians.

To compound the problem, Québec would be trying at the same time to sell many of its bonds abroad. It would not be a great time to be a bad guy. All these jurisdictional conflicts with aboriginals would play against the interests of Québec — at the precise moment of other pressing priorities — unless the Québec government wants to cede territory.

The desert crossing would be long and dry. Each problem enumerated above could be resolved if addressed in isolation. But taken together, they impose not only an additional burden, but also an unbearable multiplication. If there were only a slowdown due to anglophone discontent in Montréal, so be it. In normal times, we could also deal with a Québec dairy industry crisis or a job crisis in the Outaouais. But combine the Montréal slowdown with these crises; add a loss of confidence plus a restrictive fiscal policy; then the problems multiply rapidly.

Now let's look at each of these adjustments and their individual impacts, chapter by chapter.

7

The Farmer's Tale

David Johnston: *Traditionally we think of farmers as largely independent of political and economic fortunes. How will they be struck by this potential divorce?*

Marcel Côté: First consider their size and shape. Six thousand Québec "industrial" milk farmers produce 120 million litres annually worth $600-million. They sell to agricultural cooperatives for butter, cheese, ice cream, yogurt, and powdered milk finished products worth $2-billion.

Their market, however, is an artificial one. In 1970 Canadian producers agreed to a central marketing operation. Each province was guaranteed the market shares then held — for Québec 47%. Sale price was the *then* market price. Some years later, milk producers convinced Ottawa to close the Canadian market to imports except for an imported cheese quota. Over the years, the Canadian prices then rose to double the international price, that is, the U.S. price. With

1994's GATT agreement, tariffs will replace the national quotas. The tariff will slowly decline over the years, but the initial level will be so high that imported dairy products, especially from the United States, will remain uncompetitive.

How do Québec industrial milk producers fare with this 47% share of a protected Canadian market at twice world prices?
Strangely enough, with difficulty. It is expensive to get into business. Their "quota" for milk typically costs them $300,000 to $400,000, greater than the value of their cows. Secondly, the market is shrinking; people are drinking more and more 2%, 1%, and skim milk rather than whole milk. Milk producers have the historic right to sell the butter, drawn from whole milk, when lower percentage or skim milk is produced, into the protected industrial milk market. Thus they cannibalize their own protected enclave.

So what would happen to these farmers under separation?
First, the Ontario (the largest part of the Canadian protected market) consumer will want to stop paying twice the market price for industrial milk. Secondly, Ontario milk producers will covet the Québec quotas. Thirdly, no patriotic Ontarian will want to subsidize Québec farmers.

Within a few weeks — not months — of independence, the joint Canadian plan for industrial milk will fall apart. Failing an (unlikely) amendment to the Canadian supply management law, Québec production will be threatened first by Canadian producers experiencing tough times now claiming the Québec quotas, and second by consumers and industrial users preferring cheaper American milk. Canadian producers could double their production quotas with a temporary right of importation, either from the United States or Québec, according to the GATT rules, at international prices. Over the following years, Canadian producers will build up their herds and replace the imports.

This is a dramatic shift. How do Québec farmers react?

With mythology. First: "They are our friends," they say of Canadian farmers. But with stakes of $500-million and the break-up of Canada, friendship vanishes.

Secondly: "They could not produce enough milk without us." In fact, imports from the U.S. will fill the gap and Ontario producers will also buy bargain-priced cows from Québec to increase their own herds.

Thirdly: "They do not have enough conversion plants." But Canada could import finished products while it is increasing its transformation capacity.

Finally, the *pièce de resistance*: "We have an agreement that they would dare not break." And Canadian confederation, is that not an agreement?

In fact, with Québec separation wouldn't the entire Canadian agricultural pact dissolve?

Yes. Today the federal government spends $2-billion annually in direct subsidies and forgivable loans to western Canadian farmers. Eastern farmers receive the equivalent of $2-billion through higher prices, from protected markets for milk, poultry, and eggs. Both limbs will fall.

Some Quebec farmers threaten counter-attacks: "We'll stop buying western beef." But western beef is sold at market prices set in Chicago.

If Québecers supply themselves at market price from the United States, western producers will respond by reorienting their sales to the United States. This realignment has already begun. Beef runs increasingly on a north-south axis.

In fact, only milk, eggs, and poultry have protected markets in the world of Canadian agriculture. Production quotas for fresh milk, eggs, and poultry held by Québec farmers roughly equal Québec's consumption level. But for industrial milk the subsidy is enormous. Québec produces twice as much as it consumes. It ships the surplus elsewhere in Canada, at twice the world price. In fact, industrial milk counts for more than 90% of surplus quotas for agricultural products in Québec.

What happens when this pact ends?

A real torpedo hits. Within several weeks, Québec industrial milk producers would permanently lose half of their market. Under GATT it is illegal to ship subsidized milk into international markets. Québec converters, with several thousand workers making ice cream, cheese, and yogurt, would also lose 50% of their market. Massive layoffs would ensue.

The shock of this torpedo would reverberate across the entire Québec agricultural economy. Within a few weeks the most profitable 12% of Québec agriculture would disappear. Loss of quotas would cut one-third of milk farmers' production immediately.

Investments in quotas, frequently used as collateral for loss, would collapse. Many would fall into bankruptcy. Credit unions and rural agricultural cooperatives would suffer substantial losses.

Some would rejoice over the sad fate of the milk producers. "This

had to happen eventually. One must eliminate protected markets."
Perhaps that's true, but one does not heal the sick by hitting them on
the head with a hammer. To eliminate in several weeks half of the
industrial milk quotas is horse medicine. This will cause enormous
problems in rural areas, producing bankruptcies, plundering prices,
wrecking families. Transition to a free market should be staged. The
Québec farmers' union has proposed twenty years or more.

Is the agricultural pact unique? Are there analogous situations?
Nothing as big. But throughout Québec one finds many workers sup-
plying markets protected by Canadian political ententes. Expro of
Valleyfield and SNC Technologies at Saint-Augustin and Repentigny
would have to find new markets for their ammunition. Canadair would
lose the Armed Forces CF-12 maintenance contract (to the profit of
Winnipeg, which has waited for it for ten years). CAE, Bendix, Pratt &
Whitney, Bell Helicopters, and many other enterprises dependent on
the Canadian military order books would be hit.

***But the government of the new Québec would take over this
order book?***
Sure, but you can't suck and whistle at the same time. The Québec
government has said it wants a small army concentrated on ground
forces to cut expenditures.

Other examples?
One which would touch all Québecers is a 15% to 20% increase in
the monthly telephone bill. The federal CRTC regulates telephone
charges across Canada. It uses total Bell Canada revenues for both

Québec and Ontario to fix uniform subscriber charges across both jurisdictions. For demographic and economic reasons, there are many more long distance calls per capita in Ontario. This results in lower rates charged in Québec to equal Ontario rates. With independence, the Bell rate base would be divided in two. Québec rates would immediately increase at least 15%.

These three examples of industrial milk, military supplies, and telephones involve protected markets. Are there broader dislocations that would result from loss of economies of scale? Enormous ones. Let's illustrate by asking why prices are generally lower in the United States for manufactured products like personal computers or clothing. This occurs because businesses can spread their overhead costs over a much larger consumer population. The reverse applies when the population base is reduced — which would be the case if Québec separates.

Separatists reply that there would be a common market between Québec and Canada. After that there will be a common market between Canada and the United States because NAFTA will be continued? With free trade agreements governing Québec and Canada and Québec and North America, there will be no additional trade costs after separation. Let's return to common market and NAFTA issues later. For now let's assume the indépendantistes are right about a common market. What they ignore is the discontinuity of the legal framework. Examples include the absence of a common supreme court, the non-application of one country's laws in another, and so on. Businesses adapt by creating subsidiary corporations in the other country with full national rights, but also with separate operating costs and accounting systems, and loss of interdivisional financing and of economies of scale. This is observable between Canada and the United States today. In sum, these operating subsidiaries in other countries create significant additional costs.

Can you quantify these increased structural costs?

With difficulty. For telephones, it is at least 15%. Natural gas can anticipate an increase of 10%. An average increase of 5% in all sectors presently integrated on the Canadian scale would not be surprising. This structural hike would produce secondary price increases in the service sector, resulting in significant inflationary pushes. This would be similar to a generalized tax increase diminishing the purchasing power of all Québecers.

Aside from increased cost of living, how would individuals be affected in their daily lives?

Canada would become a foreign country, like the United States today. At the border, there would be identity controls. There would be barriers to work in Canada. A permit would be required. We would no longer hold Canadian passports. This is just the beginning.

Many people would not like this at all. In the next two chapters, we'll put under the microscope two communities — Montréal Anglo-Québecers and residents of the Outaouais — who would be greatly affected by independence. They would react very differently. Independence would devastate them.

8

The Anglo-Québecer Exodus

They represent more than one-quarter of Montréal's population: 620,000 anglophones (English as their first language) and at least 200,000 immigrants who have opted for English as their North American language. While they live in English, more than one-half of them get along well in French. Their reaction to independence will inflict on Québec's economy its biggest economic shock.

*

David Johnston: *What about the argument that most of those who would want to leave Québec have already gone? And that those anglophones who have chosen to remain here since 1976 are solidly anchored?*

Marcel Côté: This affirmation rests on two false assumptions: first, that anglophones believe that independence will not result in a major change in their status as citizens; secondly, that anglophones have patterns of mobility similar to those of francophones, particularly in times of economic crisis.

Explain the first.

Anglophones do not have the same confidence francophones have in Québec political institutions. Compare the letters to the editor columns in the *Gazette* and *La Presse*. That says it all. Anglophone attitudes to government in an independent Québec would be very different from francophone attitudes. Their comportment would also be different.

And the second?

Patterns of mobility differ. For an anglophone, moving from Montréal to Ottawa or to Toronto is comparable to a francophone moving from Sherbrooke or Québec to Montréal.

Exceptional migration of ethnic minorities is customary with political disruption. Québec would be no exception. Québec francophones, at least the majority of them, would make a choice of country. Québec anglophones would also face a choice of country.

How would that choice be exercised?

In three ways. First, one already has the normal "moving" phenomenon: young people who leave home and go to Ontario or the west for work because prospects there are better; employees whose jobs are transferred; retirees who migrate to Vancouver or Miami. Eleven thousand Anglo-Québecers and 7500 Franco-Québecers left Québec annually over the last decade. Note the basic rate of annual migration: anglophones 1 per 75; francophones 1 per 800. This gap reflects the greater inter-provincial mobility of Québec anglophones versus francophones.

Secondly, examine the reverse phenomenon: arrivals in Québec from elsewhere in Canada. Québec annually welcomes from the rest of Canada 6000 anglophones and 9000 francophones, much fewer than those who leave. Just as in 1977-80, after the election of René Lévesque's separatist government, arrivals would be radically lower in the years following independence. Québec's economic crisis would discourage immigrants.

Thirdly, departures would increase dramatically. A large percentage of Montréal anglophones say they would leave Québec after independence. This attitude is normal. Anglophones are as proud of their culture as we of ours. They have more confidence in their own institutions. They want to conserve their Canadian citizenship and confidence. Moreover, the economy will sour in Québec with threats of a yet more serious crisis to come.

The anglophones would be encouraged by their own. Just as the majority of Québec francophones in the regions have relatives and friends in Montréal, the majority of anglophones in Québec have relatives and friends elsewhere in Canada. They would see their own friends, relatives, and colleagues emigrating. An enormous pessimism would permeate the English community.

The weighing of different elements in exercising this choice would not be the same for all. Economics and emotions would factor differently. For many anglophones, Montréal is their town "for better or worse, till death us do part." The price of homes would drop, manacling some to their neighbourhoods. Young people, renters, and those without jobs would be less severely affected.

But let's look at jobs because they would determine so much else.
Right. We begin with relocation of head offices. While the immediate

head office exodus may not be as large as some Cassandras predict, the effect would be devastating. Working in these head offices are anglophones readiest to leave. With independence Montréal would abdicate its claims as a Canadian business centre; it would become a Québec business centre.

What proportion of head offices would leave?

The majority of multinationals would leave. Only some of them, well anchored in Québec, like Alcan and Bombardier, would keep their head offices here. Others would legally restructure their operations, establishing two distinct corporations: one for Canada, the other for Québec. They would adapt to the legal discontinuity created by separation, mirroring the separation of political space. Montréal would be the great loser. Only Québec operations' head offices would remain here.

Here's a list of head offices that could leave because they have a larger part of their business or shareholders outside of Québec or a higher percentage of anglophone executives, or all of the above: Canadian Pacific, Canadian National, Bell Canada and BCE, Standard Life, Imasco, Royal Bank, Air Canada, Pratt & Whitney.

Take one of these business reorganizations and explain job losses.

Pratt & Whitney Canada has its Canadian head office in Longueuil, on the south shore of Montréal. After independence, it is likely to divide into two. The Québec head office would be responsible only for the Longueuil factory. The management of the Canadian factories would report to the new Pratt & Whitney Canada head office newly located elsewhere in Canada. What percentage of their head office jobs would actually remain in Québec? Judge for yourself.

Consider the Montréal pharmaceutical sector. It would be decimated. Supervision of Canadian activities would pass from Québec subsidiaries to the new Canadian subsidiaries. Many other sectors would feel this disruption of Québec subsidiaries. The reverse would be less true: Canadian enterprises with head offices outside of Québec but important activities in Québec have already established a Québec business centre for the peculiarities of the Québec market.

What about the ripple effect across other sectors?

A great number of business services will be affected also: lawyers, accountants, communications workers, financial advisers. One specific example is pension fund managers. An important part of that industry would leave Québec simply because the government of Canada could continue to require that Canadian pension funds be administered in Canada.

Loss of business service jobs, then, could easily surpass head office job loss.

Can you quantify the structural loss of jobs in Montréal?

With precision, no. But the losses would be high, for two reasons. First, some activities, such as that of head offices, would be transferred directly. Secondly, and more gradually, many in the business sector would see their sales erode with the exodus of a significant portion of their clientele. Estimates range from 5% to 15% of some 1.4 million jobs in Montréal.

Population losses would mirror business losses. They would be deeper than during the period from 1976 to 1981. This time, there would be no false alarm. Of the 800,000 who live in English in Montréal, easily 200,000 to 300,000 could leave within a few years. There would also be francophone departures, precipitated principally by the difficult economic conditions and by the necessity to choose between Canadian and Québec citizenship. This francophone emigration encompassing, among others, many of Montréal's entrepreneurial and creative people, could reach 50,000, or 1% to 2% of the population. Globally, the Montréal region could lose 10% of its population in several years. To deny this possibility is to play ostrich.

How would one feel these losses in everyday life?

Look around you at the "built environment." The construction industry would stagnate for several years. In a normal year 10,000 apartment units are constructed in Montréal. The equivalent of five years' apartment construction would be lost after independence. Are you skeptical? Look at the Hull-Gatineau region during the 1970s. Before the victory of the Parti Québécois, 3000 houses and apartments were constructed annually. From 1977 to 1980, 100 to 200 apartments per year were constructed — 20 times less. The region's population fell 1% while Québec overall population grew 3%. During the 1980s, the number of starts returned to their historic rhythm. House construction is sensitive to population migrations.

Office construction would also be greatly affected.

Can you calculate how much?

Reliable estimates suggest one to two million square feet of vacated office buildings with the departure of head offices and related activities — equal to two Place Ville-Maries. Just as office-building construction ceased in Montréal from 1977 to 1980, there would be none in the years immediately following independence.

Montréal's construction industry employs 55,000; it would be on its back for some years. What is worse, Québec construction workers would be barred from work in Ontario, just as in the U.S. today.

Is it all loss/loss?

No. Certain segments of the Montréal population might rejoice. The French-Canadian bourgeoisie could find some good bargains in this crisis. There would be less competition for jobs in management positions. Thanks to the fall in prices of luxury houses, some Montréalers could move to Upper Westmount or West Island tranquillity. But the population in general would experience severe disadvantages. The largest losses would strike construction, commerce, and offices.

But I can hear some nationalists retorting, "Economic terrorism — you are brandishing empty threats. The same threats were uttered in 1976. Montréal survived."

They're wrong on both counts. Montréal was deeply and permanently damaged after 1976. The damage from this bomb of Québec separation would be much more devastating.

Okay, what precisely was the permanent damage to Montréal between 1976 and 1981, under the first péquiste government?

About 75,000 people, anglophones in the very large majority, left Montréal. They did not feel at home in a province led by an indépendantiste government, or they were looking for better economic conditions, the same causes that would be put into play if Québec becomes independent. By comparison with Toronto, the unemployment rate in Montréal climbed 3%, as the graph below shows. It did not budge elsewhere in the province in comparison with Ontario. Three percent unemployment — 40,000 Montréalers who lost their jobs. And that was only a false alarm.

The unemployed were not all privileged citizens of Outremont. Even though fifteen years have passed, many vividly recollect the state of the Montréal economy between 1976 and 1981. Construction collapsed. Cranes vanished from Montréal's skyline. Home starts fell from 12,000 units annually during the period 1971-76 to 4000 annually from 1976 to 1981 but stayed steady elsewhere in Québec. And along with construction workers, commercial and office workers suffered most from the economic slowdown precipitated by our political problems.

Graph 1
Relative unemployment rates

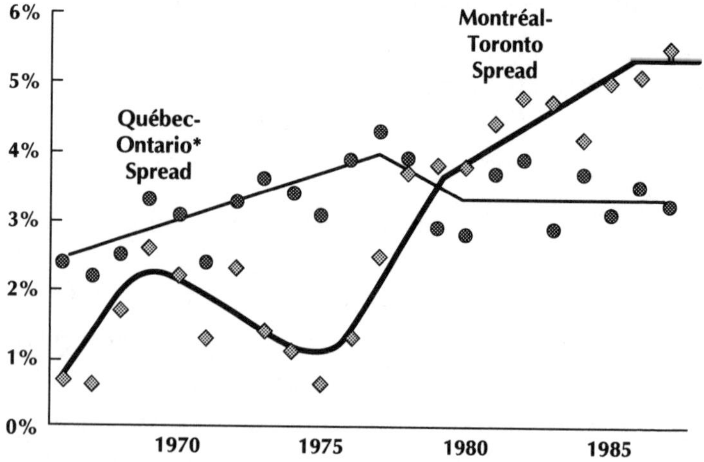

* *Outside Toronto and Montréal*

So Montréal will be the big loser if Québec separates.

Everybody in Québec will lose big as the effect of what happens in Montréal spreads to the rest of Québec. Montréal will lose an important part of its population, a significant portion of its head office activities, and what is more serious, a large slice of its brain power. More than a quarter of the population of Montréal is anglophone, proud of being so, and determined to live in its anglophone culture, in a bilingual community called Montréal, located in Québec in Canada. If one denies these opportunities to anglophones they will leave, without too much fuss as is the Anglo-Saxon way. But they will leave a gaping hole in the Montréal economy and its intellectual, social, and cultural fabric. Other Montréalers will pay the bill. The sole consolation for those who remain will be that things could have been worse. They could have lived in the Outaouais, where there will be a veritable economic massacre.

9

The Massacre in the Outaouais

David Johnston: *Why and how will Hull-Gatineau suffer?*

Marcel Côté: The Outaouais is the richest region in Québec because of federal government jobs. The index for standard of living is 107 compared with a Québec average - 100; Québec City - 102; Montréal - 97; and Abitibi - 79. Urbanized Outaouais extends from Aylmer in the west to Masson in the east but is dominated by the twin cities of Hull-Gatineau.

Its economic *raison d'être* is the national capital of Canada, Ottawa. Of 120,000 jobs, 25,000 are in the federal government (including military agencies and crown corporations) and 20,000 are in the private sector on the Ontario side.

So independence would be devastating for the Outaouais. How do separatists respond?

They concede that some jobs would certainly be lost. But the new government of Québec would make Hull-Gatineau the second capital of Québec, a place where the Québec government could locate 10,000 to 15,000 civil service jobs.

And how does that look under your microscope?

Let's use someone else's microscope. The Bélanger-Campeau Commission formed by Québec's National Assembly retained a group of consultants to analyse all the federal ministries. Their mission: to determine what federal jobs Québec ought to conserve after independence and where these jobs could be located. They concluded the Hull region would only lose 8195 government jobs, 10% of the region's jobs. This number could even diminish if the Québec government transferred some civil service department or government agencies from Québec City to Hull.

Are these estimates realistic?

Let's perform a little exercise together. First, understand the nature of the federal jobs in Hull. As Table 3 shows, the federal government employs 216,000 civil servants and 55,000 militia across the entire country. There's an obvious concentration in the national capital region. National Defence and armed forces' employees and the Royal

Table 3
Federal government personnel

Regions	Civil servants		Defence, RCMP		Total
	000	%	000	%	
National capital					
Ontario	54.1	25.0	8.7	15.6	62.8
Québec	18.0	8.3	1.3	2.3	19.3
Subtotal	72.1	33.3	10.0	18.0	82.1
Québec	33.0	15.2	4.8	8.6	37.8
Elsewhere in Canada	111.3	51.4	39.8	71.6	151.1
Total	216.4	100.0	55.6	100.0	272.0

Source: Treasury Board; armed forces are excluded

Canadian Mounted Police are categorized separately. The RCMP performs provincial police duties in eight provinces. Employees of crown corporations such as Canada Post, CN, and CBC are also excluded.

Let's organize governmental activities into two categories. *Head office* activities — for instance, of ministers and deputy-ministers — are concentrated in the national capital. They represent 33% of the personnel (excluding defence and the RCMP). *Service* activities — for instance, Canada Manpower Centres, regional tax offices, and parks — are distributed everywhere across the country. Table 3 indicates that, excluding defence and the RCMP, Québec accounts for 33,000 of all these jobs, or 23.5% of the whole. Québec has only 9% of the defence and the RCMP jobs, which are concentrated in the Maritime provinces and in the west, reflecting the provincial police mandates of the RCMP (paid for by the provinces served) and armed force base prominence in Atlantic Canada. Globally, excluding defence and RCMP personnel, Québec has its just proportion (23.5%) of federal personnel, within 1.5% of its share of the total population.

In the national capital region, a quarter of the civil servants work on the Québec side. One quarter of civil servants are also residents of the Outaouais. In sum, the federal government reflects the national average, in jobs and place of residence.

And if Québec becomes independent?

The Québec government would take over the regional service activities in Québec. Most, if not all, of the federal civil servants working in the regions (including Montréal) would be transferred into the Québec public service. But what would happen to the 20,000 "head office" civil servants residing in the Outaouais? The Québec government could decide to locate some displaced "head office" activities in Hull, in the buildings evacuated by the government of Canada, in place of repatriating them to Québec City. Those activities which remain in the Outaouais, and activities relocated from Québec to Hull, would create some jobs for the former federal civil servants.

But how many?

Not many, for three reasons. First, government head office activities are generally concentrated around the political centre, here Québec City. Take, for example, the Québec equivalent to the Canadian International Development Agency (CIDA). This agency must be located near the government seat. It's an important instrument of foreign policy. Take the national archives. They must be located in proximity to the centre of government for easy consultation. In fact, only the management of self-governing agencies, for example, health insurance (which is already in Québec), pension authority (already in Montréal and Québec), tax collection (already partly decentralized) may be easily located far from the capital. This limits the number of head office activities which could remain in Hull after independence. Other ministries will be thinned to eliminate duplications, the obsession of indépendantistes.

And reason two?

Consider the occupational profile of the federal civil servants resident in the Outaouais. Many would not have the qualifications for the "new" jobs. For example, they include relatively few senior civil servants. On the other hand, they do comprise many technical specialists. But a research centre doesn't function by putting a molecular chemistry specialist to work side by side with an economic statistician. Also, one finds a surplus of clerical employees among the federal civil servants resident in the Outaouais.

And the third reason?

Difficulties in transferring governmental activities from one city to another. For twenty years, governments in Canada have tried to devolve certain activities out of the capital region. Evaluate the results. Modest decentralization, due partly to collective agreement rigidities but also to difficulties in transferring administrative activities *en bloc*. It is even difficult to transfer activities within the same region. Some years ago, the government attempted to transfer several hundred functionaries from Parliament Hill in Québec City to Charlebourg, a suburb situated less than ten kilometres away. It succeeded only after exhausting debate. To transfer thousands from Québec City to Hull would be a task eminently more arduous.

Are there good examples of a second administrative capital?

No. Montréal has long claimed head office jobs from the Québec government. For twenty years Québec premiers have spent more time in Montréal than Québec. However, no more than several hundred head office jobs have actually been transferred. A single deputy-minister is located in Montréal. Victoria and Vancouver, Edmonton and Calgary, Albany and New York, these show the same pattern. There's only one capital. Logic supports the concentration of a government's head office activities into the capital city.

Can you put the proposed second capital of Québec under your own microscope?

Yes. In 1991, for the account of a consultative committee set up in the Outaouais to assess the impact of separation, we estimated the potential government jobs that the government of Québec could conserve in the Outaouais after independence. We reviewed each federal and provincial ministry, concentrating on head office activities that could be located in the Outaouais. Including the armed forces, the most optimistic total was 10,000 jobs, including significant relocation of activities currently located in Québec City. A more realistic estimate is 5000 jobs. In sum, the loss of public service jobs is 15,000 if you are optimistic — 20,000 if you are more prudent.

Could the Québec residents conserve their jobs with the federal side?

For one or two years, perhaps, but no longer than a reasonable time it would take to relocate their place of residence. In fact, the Canadian government would undertake massive layoffs to adjust its size to a population suddenly diminished by 25%. They would give preference to Canadian citizens. It would be abnormal for a government to employ citizens of foreign countries on its own territory while facing serious problems of unemployment. Charity begins at home.

But that's not all! Remember border posts. To work in Ontario a Québecer would need a work permit. This change of status would skewer part-time and seasonal workers, and particularly construction workers. Construction employs several thousand people in the Outaouais working principally in Ontario. Five thousand to 10,000 Outaouais residents working in Ontario would lose their jobs, 25% to 50% of the total of these jobs.

The Massacre in the Outaouais

Can you put this blow to the Outaouais economy into a broader context?

With 20,000 to 30,000 basic jobs lost, a 50% diminution of the urban region's economic base, the region's *raison d'être* would evaporate. Service sector employment would atrophy. Construction would stagnate. Numerous public servants would move to Ontario to keep their jobs, thus vacating numerous lodgings. Large numbers would also quit the region for more economically clement places. Certain office towers in central Hull would simply be abandoned.

The region's urban centre's population of 150,000 would drop dramatically. Employment, now at 120,000, could drop to 70,000. Hull-Gatineau would echo Sept-Iles. There the economic base withered in the early 1980s. Here the shock would be bigger. In fact, there could be no future in the Outaouais until a new vocation was invented. That would take decades, at the best.

Can you cite other border-city examples?

Twin cities juxtaposed along borders generally are oddly suited couples. Detroit and Windsor; Laredo, Texas, and Nueva Laredo, Mexico; San Diego and Tijuana; and in smaller towns, Edmunston, in New Brunswick, and Madawaska, Maine. The cross-border couple is always in disequilibrium. There's a rich and a poor town.

The future of Hull and Gatineau in an independent Québec would not be enviable. Go to Rouyn or Rimouski. These are proud towns, but also towns where the economic base is similar to Hull and Gatineau in an independent Québec: they are towns that are smaller, less wealthy, and, unfortunately, facing major employment problems. Hull and Gatineau in an independent Québec would be far from first place.

10

Divorce and Recession

David Johnston: *Let's recapitulate. The region of Montréal, the urban region of the Outaouais, milk producers, and defence workers would be most affected economically by the transition into independence. What would this mean in economic terms for the new Québec?*

Marcel Côté: Taken alone, each of these economic torpedoes could not cause a recession. Taken together the effect is devastating. But additional causes drive the recession that would follow the constitutional divorce.

What are these?

Let us first identify sectors that would *not* be touched by the transition to independence. The natural resource sector is oriented to exports outside of Canada. Pulp and paper plants, aluminum refineries, mines, and smelters, and the towns that depend on these industries would not be directly hit. Cities such as Sept-Iles, Baie-Comeau, and Alma should not be immediately affected by the transition, either in services or industry. In certain respects, a two-speed Québec would emerge. For a time, the outlying regions, beneficiaries of natural resources, would not be affected. But the centre of Québec, between Montréal and Québec, more oriented towards manufactured products and services and towards Montréal, would beat at a subdued pulse.

Manufacturing enterprises that export would continue to do so. But they would feel the transition more, particularly if sales to Canada represent an important part of their production. There would be a "backlash" from Canadian industrial buyers and consumers. One can deny this. But even today salespeople covering the rest of Canada recite "backlash" incidents. Attitudes would harden during the transition.

Québecers would be accused of breaking up the country, mistreating their minorities, misinterpreting obligations to aboriginals, and so on. They would also be blamed for English Canada's recession.

Divorces usually affect both spouses' financial situation. Generally, it's the same for divorces of countries. An exception is the Czech Republic, which surged ahead following divorce from Slovakia.

Could this be the case for Canada in its divorce from Québec?
Probably not. First, exports from Canada to Québec would be reduced because of Québec's economic crisis. What is more, as we will see further on, the Canadian economy would suffer from the restrictive monetary policy following Québec's separation, which would lead to an economic slowdown.

But back to the effects on Québec.
Enterprises drawing significant revenues from the Montréal economy

would be battered by this region's problems. Many small and medium enterprises located everywhere across Québec would suffer from the ricochet of the Montréal economic malaise.

Private investments would also be severely touched by the transition. Uncertainty about the economic prognosis would not be the sole cause of hesitation among investors. In fact, greater uncertainty may derive from the ill-defined legal framework in which Québec will find itself for a number of years. Changing status — from province of Canada to independent country — requires renegotiation of many agreements. Some are treaties that must be approved by legislatures; some are complex multi-country agreements like NAFTA and GATT.

What are the mechanics of renegotiating treaties?

Let's take tax treaties. A country like Québec must negotiate at least 30 fiscal treaties with its new commercial partners. Each fiscal treaty would be specific and different. Tax laws vary from one country to another. One does not simply rewrite the Canadian treaty; the fiscal regime of an independent Québec would be different from the rest of Canada. Québec would be a unitary regime and not a federal regime with two levels of taxation. Each country with whom Québec negotiates a fiscal treaty would have its own calendar of negotiations, with its own demands. Countries most significant for Québec, like Canada, the United States, France, Great Britain, Holland, and the Bahamas, may have other priorities. Finally, the government of Québec would not have a team of unlimited size to renegotiate these treaties.

But NAFTA would be the most important?

Yes and perhaps the most difficult. It would require the agreement of Canada, Mexico, and the American congress, which is likely to become immersed in aboriginal issues. Lobby groups would attack subsidies to our film industry and regional development. Although Québec would probably ultimately be accepted in NAFTA, approval delays might be long and exact painful compromises. Provisions applying to a different country are not the same as those applying to a province. Meanwhile, some "protective" American industries would seek to profit from the disappearance of dispute resolution panels to make life difficult for our exporters. Ask Québec lumber and pork exporters how harassing the Americans can be when trade arbitration panels are ineffective.

Aside from NAFTA, what other country-to-country kinds of things must be done?

First, the recognition of the laws of Québec elsewhere in Canada, and vice versa, would require negotiations with each of the provinces and some modifications of their laws as well as ours. Then, there are environmental ententes, principally with the United States. These would demand complex renegotiations. They would be tripartite. There would also be commercial agreements. Over the course of the years Canada has signed many of these with different countries. They are profitable to Québec enterprises. It would be necessary to review these agreements, which were signed with Canada, contact the countries implicated, and sit down and renegotiate them, with or without amendments.

How long does all this legal reordering take?

Impossible to predict. First, Québec would not proceed onto the field with a normal country's legal framework, even if it declared itself independent. Lawyers with the Bélanger-Campeau Commission focused on Québec's international recognition as a sovereign country. They concluded that the succession from province to country could take place in an orderly manner. But even if they are right, there is much more to seek than simply the recognition of the juridical order of the country, particularly when it comes to international relations. The operating framework is defined by a large group of treaties negotiated with a multitude of countries. One can not simply rewrite the Canadian ententes. The other countries must acquiesce.

Québec does not possess Canada's negotiating cards. Some years would pass before there would be a sufficient package of treaties and ententes to carry on our international affairs. Our diplomats would be flooded with details. That would limit our ability to move quickly. Meanwhile, uncertainty would reign. How will investors repatriate their profits? What interest rates will prevail in Québec? Are there guarantees? What to do in the absence of a clear response? One waits. Investors would wait — which would have the anticipated negative impact on the Québec economy.

Québec industry would also be on pins and needles. Businesspeople would simply test the waters of the new economy before plunging into investments. One cannot ignore the psychological impact of border posts, perturbations in early years by zealous civil servants, risks arising from temporary uncertainties regarding NAFTA, failures in finding sufficient foreign partners to reconstitute a critical mass of international ententes.

But you give no credit to the enthusiasm and élan of Québecers newly masters of their own house.

That argument is, at least in the short term, unfounded. Businesses would be thrown off balance by the amplitude of their tasks, the economy's depressing state, and new obstacles that have emerged. There would be some enthusiasts. But few of them would be industrialists. In the longer term, the tonic of transition to a new country could perhaps have a stimulating effect. People eventually learn to overcome adversity by their own means. But it is decidedly preferable to avoid the adversity in advance.

In fact, the business world would simply pace down during the transition. The hibernation of private investment would be conditioned as much by the drop in internal demand as by the uncertainty resulting from the incomplete legal framework of a newly independent country.

Can you give an overall assessment of this recession?
Never, anywhere, have I seen as many negative factors converge as in this prospective newly independent Québec economy. These are real shocks, the sum of which is exceptional. They can create a recession unlike any Québec has ever seen. One can easily envisage some 200,000 to 300,000 additional unemployed and more, triggered specifically by the problems of Montréal, rural Québec, and the Outaouais, but extended more broadly by the slowdown in the Canadian economy, inflationary pressures, and a fall in private investment.

But the new government of Québec would have the tools of a country. Can it not use these tools to deflect this recession?
Let us analyse this Québec and its tools on the day after independence with a simple family story.

11

Obese and Beggar Governments

Paul and Virginia are in good health. But they have a "little" problem. Both weigh about 50 pounds more than they should. Fortunately, as their doctor emphasizes on their annual physical examination, their hearts are in good shape. This encourages them to live well and particularly to overeat.

Paul and Virginia are well aware of their weight problem. But they enjoy good food too much. No diet has succeeded. They can afford a good tailor who succeeds more often than not in masking the extra poundage. Each year their doctor advises them to modify their eating habits. But in vain. Paul and Virginia are *bon vivants*. Paul blames Virginia. Virginia blames Paul. Nothing more is done.

Except for last week. Paul and Virginia presented themselves for their annual examination. No change as far as weight. But Paul drops a bomb: "Doctor, this weight problem doesn't make sense any more. Virginia and I have decided to take a big step. Next week we'll run the Montréal marathon. That will solve our weight problem!"

The doctor was shocked. He thought: "They are crazy. I have never seen two persons in as bad physical condition dare to think of tackling a marathon. They are not trained. They are going to die!" But then he thought, "They could not run half a kilometre before gasping for air. They will learn their lesson. Perhaps then they will decide to change their eating habits and to run their marathon when they are in shape!"

*

David Johnston: *How does this apply to Canada and Québec?*
Marcel Côté: If there were doctors who watched over the debt weight of countries, they would diagnose similarly in the case of Québec and Canada who have just announced their marathon — the intention to separate into two countries. "They are crazy!" they would say. Then, revising their opinion, they would conclude: "Let them bicker. They will come back to their senses as soon as they examine their physiques and the rigours of the 26-mile marathon. But first they must discover their condition!"

Canada and Québec have governments indebted to the limit. They are among the most indebted in the world — like Paul and Virginia with their 50 extra pounds. They blame one another. But both are to blame. While they bicker about blame, they persist in their bad habits.

How do the debts of Québec and Canada compare with other jurisdictions?

Note in Table 4 the debt and deficit for Québec and Canada as a whole, compared with other large industrial countries. (The classification was done by the OECD, an international organization, using a statistical base slightly different than ours.) Canada has the worst combination of debt and deficit after a sick Italy (which to its credit has a lot of domestic savings to pay for its excesses — not the case for us). Québec is slightly worse than Canada, by about 10%.

Another of Québec's peculiarities is how much it depends on foreign loans for 54% of the debt it issues or guarantees. Québec is one of the biggest foreign borrowers in New York! Canada also began some years ago to borrow from foreigners in a big way. The other provinces also do it. This dependence on foreign capital to finance our government's dietetic disequilibriums is expensive. Last year Canada paid $35-billion in interest and dividends to foreign investors who have advanced funds to us. This is $1200 for each Canadian. The figure is worse for Québecers. Interest and dividends paid out of Québec to foreign bond holders in 1994 exceeds $10-billion, or $1500 dollars per citizen.

Table 4
Obese and beggar governments

	Public debt % of GDP	Government deficit % of GDP
Canada		
National average	92	7.1
Québec	104	8.0
United States	69	2.0
France	44	3.3
Japan	75	2.0
Italy	123	9.6
Belgium	146	6.6

Sources: OECD; Departments of Finance, Québec, Canada 1993

Why do we have this weight problem?

As with Paul and Virginia, a lack of discipline: our governments' inability to correct their annual deficits. In this respect we are among the worst governments in the world. Each year, our governments run a deficit. Our debt increases. The expenditure to finance the debt continues to mount. In 1994, 24% of federal government expenditures was devoted to servicing the debt. In Québec, 13%. In fact, the annual deficits of the two governments are equal to their debt-service cost.

The Canada and Québec deficit problems are profound. Nothing is gained by blaming one government more than another. The two are to blame. In fact, we the taxpayers are to blame. We re-elect politicians who perpetuate a policy of overeating. We oppose deficit reduction measures, particularly when they affect us personally.

Can you show this in more detail?

Table 5 presents the 1993 budgets of Canada and Québec, presented on a per capita base. Note four things.

First, observe the importance of health, education, and transfers to individuals, which includes old-age pensions, unemployment insurance, welfare, and family allowances. Each time governments try to cut these expenditures, cries of outrage arise. Fear overcomes our politicians. It paralyses them.

Second, grants to businesses primarily serve regional development. They also make up for deficits in crown corporations, like CBC and Central Mortgage and Housing Corporation.

Third, Québec's operational deficit shows that Québec borrows to pay for groceries, that is, for regular operating expenses. It has persisted in this for twenty years, in spite of five successive premiers who denounced the practice before their election. Take a close look, especially, at the importance of the debt cost: it continues to grow year by year.

Finally, note that Québec receives $1000 per capita in federal transfers while the federal government distributes $1431 per capita. The gap masks a complex reality, the inter-regional transfers in Canadian federalism.

Table 5
Our deficit problem

($ per capita, 1994-95)

	Federal	Québec
Taxes	4265	3958
Transfers from the federal government		1000
Total, revenues	**4265**	**4958**
Transfers to provinces	938	
Federal transfers to individuals	1431	
Grants to business and farmers	703	
Education		1294
Health		1370
National Defence	372	
Other operating expenditures	634	2318
Total, operating expenditures	**4079**	**4982**
Debt service	1555	761
Budget deficit for the year	**1368**	**785**

Sources: Federal and Québec budgets, 1994-95

***This raises the fundamental question: Do Québecers receive
more from Ottawa in the form of expenditures, transfers, and
subventions than they pay in the form of taxes?***
Clearly yes, but in part because Ottawa has a deficit. All the provinces, save for British Columbia, receive more.

***Okay, let us correct for the deficit. Does Québec still receive
proportionally more from Ottawa than it pays, after having
assumed its part of the deficit?***
The response is still yes, as in fact Table 6 shows. Not much, but the
balance is nevertheless positive. It varies from year to year, fluctuat-
ing around $3-billion, or 2% of national revenue.

***Then with or without inclusion of the deficit, Québec receives
more than it gives to Canada?***
Yes.

But why is there confusion on this issue?
Some indépendantiste leaders suggest that Québec receives less from
Ottawa than Québecers pay in taxes and duty, after correction for our
part of the deficit, citing to this effect official statistics. What these
statistics confuse is how one should treat the interest expenses on the
debt. Although Québec represents 25% of the population, Québecers
receive only 21% of the interest paid by the federal government on its
debt. Is this unjust? Of course not. Québecers, for diverse reasons,
purchase fewer government of Canada bonds than the average Canadian. Québecers invest their money elsewhere. In these federal

Table 6

Who gets, who pays

Distribution of federal receipts and expenditures by regions, 1992

	Atlan.	Qué.	Ont.	Man., Sask., Terr.	Alb., B.C.	Total
Revenues (%)	6	22	41	9	22	100
Program spending (%)	14	25	32	12	18	100
Net ($-bil.)	10.7	3.3	-13.0	4.3	-5.4	—
per capita ($)	4496	463	-1250	1940	-884	—

Sources: Provincial economic accounts (Statistics Canada), Public Accounts of Canada

government statistics this appears as one less expenditure from the government of Canada to Québec.

André Raynault, the former president of the Economic Council of Canada, underlines correctly that one cannot blame the federal government for the fact that Québecers buy fewer of its bonds and its treasury bills. But the consequence is important because of the amplitude of the Canadian government's debt. The gap between our purchases of bonds and our population signifies that the federal government distributes to Québec less in interest payments than it would if we held our "population's share" of the federal debt. If we eliminate interest expenditures, it is crystal clear that Québec receives more than it gives to Ottawa, as Table 6 shows.

Can you summarize this "who loses, who gains" picture so a non-economist can understand it?

Let's try. If we separate, we wouldn't improve our fiscal situation by repatriating our taxes and expenditures. We return later to this important point. We would acquire our part of the federal debt and of the federal deficit. We would also leave in Ottawa about $3.3-billion per year, or $450 to $500 per citizen, the surplus that Québecers today realize in their transactions with the federal government.

Let us emphasize, though, that this surplus is small in comparison with that realized by the citizens of the other so-called "have-not" provinces, as Table 6 indicates. Take Atlantic Canada. Their residents contribute 6% of federal revenues but receive 14% of Ottawa spending. The net benefit that they derived from this arrangement in 1992 was $10.7-billion per year, or $4496 for every man, woman, and child in Atlantic Canada. Saskatchewan and Manitoba are also net recipients along with the Territories, together for an average of $1940 in 1992. Residents of Ontario, on the other hand, have contributed 41% of Ottawa revenues, and receive 32% of its spending, for a net contribution of $13-billion that year, or about $1250 per citizen. Alberta and B.C. are also net contributors, although at a lower level than Ontario.

This is the reality of Canadian fiscal federalism. Rich provinces support poorer provinces where the per capita revenue is below the national average. This is normal in a democracy. Examine statistics on taxes and expenditures by region in Québec. The same applies: rich regions contribute more than they receive; poorer regions receive more than they contribute. The math is similar in all the world's industrialized countries who have progressive fiscal regimes. Québec is slightly under the Canadian average as confirmed by a truckload of statistics. Assume the Canadian average per capita disposable income is 100; then Québec's per capita income is 93, and Ontario's is 109.

Can you explain this by bringing in the wealthier provinces?

In 1992 there were 350,000 Canadian taxpayers who earned taxable revenues exceeding $75,000. They paid 40% of the federal taxes in Canada. Two-thirds of these taxpayers lived in the three richest provinces in Canada: Ontario, Alberta, and British Columbia. They count for 58% of the population. But in spite of its 25% of the Canadian population, Québec has only 17% of these higher-earning taxpayers with higher revenues. The remaining provinces, with 17% of the population, have 16% of these richer taxpayers. Because people with higher revenues pay more taxes, the Canadian system becomes regionally redistributive. These are the bare facts: Québecers receive more from the federal government than they give, after adjusting for the deficit.

But aren't there many Québecers who believe the exact opposite?

Yes. Their illusions are deftly fed by those interested in spreading the myth that Québec is exploited in the federal regime. There are numerous valid reasons to criticize the federal regime, such as duplications, centralization, endless bickering. But the Canadian fiscal regime is progressive like that of Québec, the U.S., France, England, Germany. The consequence of this progressive character is well known: regions where the average revenue lags behind the national average receive more than they contribute fiscally; vice-versa for the richer regions.

It is undeniable that the average revenue in Québec is slightly under the Canadian average. Québec is situated in fourth place among Canadian provinces, on the per capita revenue index, after British Columbia, Alberta, and Ontario. One need not be Einstein or an economist to understand this. A simple tourist who visits the Canadian provinces observes the evident gradation of revenues and national wealth and the relative position of Québec.

So can one say the costs of separation to Québec are several billion dollars annually?

Far more than that. If we separate, we will have financial problems eminently more serious than this loss of some $3.3-billion. The two most important problems that we will inherit from the federal government will be our part of the annual deficit and of the federal debt. Remember Paul and Virginia. Their problem of excessive weight lasted for some years.

All right, let's look at the problem of fiscal diet and excess accumulated over the years.

It is a bad habit acquired over at least 25 years. The growth in our level of public spending exceeds that of the wealth-generating capacity of our economy and of the taxes collected to pay for the spending. Today the federal government spends $132 for every $100 it receives in taxes. It has not improved significantly over the past years. The federal government deficit is 5% of national product, one of the worst performances in the world. In spite of earnest annual budget speeches by ministers of finance, the problem of the unbalanced diet remains. It is politically difficult for governments to change their diets. The Québec government has also had an unbalanced diet for more than twenty years. We also suffer paralysis in changing our habits in adjusting our spending down to our wealth-generating base. Separation will bring Québecers the draconian regime of combining the unbalanced federal deficit with our own unbalanced deficit.

But we will also combine our debts. What obesity! The federal debt is $546-billion; one-quarter represents $136-billion. One cannot determine the exact amount of the debt we would inherit, because there would be negotiations with the federal government if we separated. Everyone agrees on current overall figures. But there is no agreement on respective responsibilities.

What are the most likely results of the negotiations?

A very difficult question to answer except that the process will be arduous. Three problems in particular will arise.

First, what is the exact amount of the debt? Should we subtract the debt held by the Bank of Canada? What about the assets of the federal government? What to say about pension funds of current federal employees?

Second, what percentage will we inherit? Our percentage of taxes (21%)? The economy (23%)? The population (25%) The past expenditures of the federal government (27%)? The stakes are high: each 1% is equivalent to $5-billion. Despite these stakes, the agreement must be politically acceptable to both sides.

Third, projects under way and ongoing liabilities have enormous financial implications. Canada is obliged to deposit money with the World Bank. Must Québec take its part? Canada is obliged to give compensation to the aboriginal peoples. Must Québec pay its part? There is $100-billion at stake in these liabilities. Canadian negotiators will insist that Québec take its share before leaving.

Are there persuasive opinions on the share of debt?

It depends on your point of view. Several studies have examined the question of the Canadian debt. The Bélanger-Campeau Commission presented the opening position of Québec in 1992: 18.5% of the federal debt. In 1994 their calculation yielded a debt of $114-billion. The Fraser Institute developed a plausible opening position for Canada: $150-billion. Gordon Gibson proposes in his book *Plan B* an amount of $135-billion or 25%, Québec's population share, but with very generous terms as to time over which this would be repaid.

All these estimates, quite different from one another, are supported by very complex analyses. Each has its own logic. But evidently, at day's end, one figure would remain: somewhere between $114- and $150-billion. Negotiators always end up in compromise. For analytical purposes, we chose $135-billion as the more plausible result of negotiations. To this amount, we must add the actual debt of the government of Québec: $45-billion at the end of 1994. Assuming independence at the end of 1994, the net debt of the Québec government (without Hydro-Québec) is $180-billion. This is 8% more than Québec's $166-billion Gross National Product (GNP) for the same year. This governmental obesity represents a debt of almost $25,000 per citizen. Over 45% would be held by foreigners, a world record for a public debt.

12

The Booty from Ottawa

David Johnston: *Assuming negotiations with Ottawa get started, what would Québec seek and what can it expect to get?*

Marcel Côté: Just as the 1980 referendum question said, Québec would expect to repatriate from Ottawa all the taxes that Québecers pay to it. Equally, the expenditures that the federal government undertakes for Québecers, would cease. Also, before leaving, Québec would have to settle the accounts for the debt and for ongoing liabilities.

Get yourself ready for a large accounting exercise, somewhat on the dry side. Counting money and debts can seem arid, but the "booty" is too important for negligence in calculations. In this chapter I will identify what could be transferred to Québec. In the following chapter I shall do surgery, eliminating the duplications and cutting the waste. This chapter is a departure and not a finishing point.

The federal government's budget is composed of revenues and expenditures.

Revenues come principally from taxes. But revenues also come from certain charges and royalties, monies from sale of permits, for example. Our attribution rule is simple. Québec gets all the revenues obtained from Québec taxpayers or payers, including premiums paid to the Unemployment Insurance Commission. Origin of the cheques determines revenues.

Expenditures break down into three categories: transfers, operations, and debt service. Transfers are payments by cheques to individuals, enterprises, or institutions such as school boards, and subordinate governments, like provinces and municipalities, according to pre-established programs and agreements. Welfare, subsidies to business and to public transport, are transfers. Transfers constitute by far the most important category of expenditure for modern governments. Our rule of destination applies. All transfer cheques destined for Québec, to the government of Québec, to businesses and institutions in Québec, or to Québec citizens, including unemployment benefits, are transfers to be allocated to Québec.

And operational expenditures?

There are the monies spent by ministries to pay their public servants, to pay rents and furnishings, and to satisfy their mandate: construction of roads or airports, defending Canada, overseas peacekeeping, in the case of the army, and so on. These monies pay for services the federal government furnishes to Canadians. In practice, negotiations between the two governments would focus on the division of civil servants. Thus Québec would take on directly certain operational expenditures while the federal government could unilaterally lower its expenditures. We simply assign 25% of these to Québec, our share of the Canadian population. In the following chapter we can identify duplications incorporated in this 25% portion.

And the third category, debt service?

This is interest payments to holders of obligations issued by the government. Remarkably, in Canada debt service has become larger over time than operational expenditures. Negotiations on federal debt sharing would determine the interest expenses inherited by the Québec government. First, the amount of debt is established. Then the rate of interest is struck. The deficit is calculated by subtracting expenditures from revenues. In 1994-95, the deficit budgeted by the federal government was $39.7-billion. A more refined deficit calculation subtracts operational expenditures, without including interest expense, from revenues. The result is called the operational deficit. Table 7 presents the federal government budget for 1994-95, our reference year for the portion of the federal operational budget attributable to Québec before all cuts or rationalizations.

Okay, let's analyse the features of this table that determine allocation of revenues and expenditures to Québec.

The budgeted revenues for the federal government for the year were $123.7-billion. The origin of the federal government revenues by province is precisely known. Based on preceding years, one can estimate (within 0.2%) that 21% of the federal government revenues come from Québec. We thus attribute $26-billion to Québec. When Mr. Parizeau speaks of recapturing our taxes from Ottawa, he refers to this $26-billion pot of gold.

Now let's turn to the other half of the question: the expenditures attributable to Québec.

A transfer expenditure is a cheque. Thus the destination of federal transfer expenses is precisely known because they occur through cheques. Cheques are distributed to persons and organizations with a precise address. Again, based on preceding years, we attribute $4.8-billion to Québec, for transfer to Québec citizens, organizations, and enterprises, and to the Québec government.

Many of these transfer expenditures are made in the framework of federal-provincial agreements. One may avoid excessive attention to the percentages that Québec receives for specific categories of transfer, as they do not take into account certain particular fiscal ententes between Québec and Canada, such as transfer of tax points. These diminish both taxes from Québec to the federal government and transfers from the federal government to Québec.

That covers transfers. Let's turn to the second category: operational expenditures.

For operational expenditures, distribution of cheques is not a good indicator. The expenditures measure the distribution of resources rather than the distribution of services received. For example, the Department of National Defence spends his budget a little bit everywhere in the world, and in Canada, proportionally more in the Atlantic provinces. Nevertheless, the resulting service of national defence is offered to all Canadians and therefore to all Québecers. Québec's portion is thus 25%. Many will say that defence spending is far too high. That is why, in the next chapter, we will tackle the cuts in these expenses. But before cutting, it is necessary to establish Québec's share.

The operational expenditures of the Canadian government were budgeted at $29.2-billion, of which $10.8-billion was for defence and $18.4-billion for the rest. Thirteen billion dollars of this $18.4-billion

Table 7
Dividing the federal budget

| | Total | Québec share | |
	$	%	$
Revenues	123.7	21.4	26.5
Transfers			
To governments	27.2	26.3	7.2
To individuals	41.5	26.0	10.8
Others	20.4	20.1	4.1
Subtotal	**89.1**	**24.8**	**22.1**
Operating expenditures			
Defence	10.8	25.0	2.7
All other	18.4	25.0	4.6
Subtotal	**29.2**	**25.0**	**7.3**
Total, program spending	118.3	25.1	29.4
Operating surplus	5.4	n.a.	(2.9)
Debt service	45.1	n.a.	n.a.
Budget deficit	39.7	n.a.	n.a.

Sources: Federal budget, 1994-95; provincial economic accounts, Statistics Canada

pays public servants, leaving $5-billion for purchase of furnishings and services, the construction of buildings, and so on. Following our share of population rule, we attribute 25% of these common expenses to Québec.

This amount, $7.3-billion, represents Québec's part of the cost of services that Ottawa furnishes to all Canadians. This doesn't imply that 25% of these expenditures are made in Québec. Québec does not receive that "just" part of federal operational expenditures. An important part of the federal services are located in Ottawa, where the head office of the Canadian government is situated. But this doesn't change the cost of these services. If Québecers want the same level of services, the bill will be 25% of federal expenditures, before adjusting for economies of scale and eliminating duplications. One-quarter of the federal government's operations expenditures is thus a good estimate for the cost of activities that Québec could repatriate. In the following chapter we will adjust this total to take account, on the one hand, of the losses of economies of scale, and on the other hand, of the elimination of duplications and reduction of some expenses.

Let's tackle the next line, the operating deficit.

Québec records an operational deficit of $2.9-billion in the federal system, while Canada in its entirety records an operational surplus of $5.4-billion, as Table 7 indicates. This difference stems from the proportionally lower revenues that the federal government draws from Québec. In fact, seven provinces out of ten, as well as the territories, are in deficit to Ottawa, because of a lower than average level of taxes paid by them to Ottawa. Three provinces — Ontario, Alberta, and British Columbia — are in surplus, for the opposite reason. These revenues reflect essentially the distribution of wealth among the provinces and the progressive character of our system of taxation.

Now we come to the toughest question of all: the debt that Québec will inherit from Ottawa.

In the previous chapter we discussed the experts' profound divergence on what Québec would owe to the rest of Canada if it withdrew from the Canadian federation. Probably after much "toing and froing" officials would adopt a Solomonic solution and cut the positions down the middle. Nevertheless, this would be one of the acrimonious tussles between Canada and Québec.

Table 8 shows two estimates of this debt. The first used the method developed by researchers of the Bélanger-Campeau Commission, favourable to Québec. The second is by the Fraser Institute, favourable to the rest of Canada. To facilitate comparisons, we apply the method of the Bélanger-Campeau Commission to the 1994-95 year. Note that we distinguish between the financial debt, assets, and what we call other liabilities, that is to say obligations arising from ongoing engagements.

This is a very complicated table. Will the negotiations be equally complicated?

Yes and no. Each point of divergence would occupy the negotiators for months of discussions. The two parties would dwell on these for good reason. Each would affirm that it does not exaggerate. It's like a divorce when it is necessary to divide assets and liabilities. But ultimately, one must compromise.

And what principle would produce a compromise?

A very simple one. The final decision must be a compromise that is politically acceptable to voters on both sides. In other words, both Québec and Canadian taxpayers would have to be willing to accept the compromise. Politics, not accountants, would determine the final outcome. There might be more room for accountants to be creative — because the electorates will not understand — about the method of

Québec's reimbursement of the debt it would inherit. The two parties have powerful arguments to defend their respective positions. But let us not embark on the debate here. For most of the elements, there is no absolute rule for decision. Each party can claim to be right. And that is one reason it will not be a simple or short negotiation.

All right, but what would the principal points of disagreement be?
Québec would not recognize many of the "other liabilities" proposed by the Fraser Institute. Canada would not agree to subtract the value of non-financial assets from the debt: each country should keep the assets it has on its territories. A major fight will erupt over the assets of the Bank of Canada. The Fraser Institute emphasizes that the Bank of Canada belongs to Canada and is not to be shared. If Québec wishes to use the Canadian dollar, so be it. But it should not realize, directly or indirectly, the benefits of "seigneurage" — the profits from issuing non-interest-bearing money. In separating, Québec should withdraw only its part of the capital share of the Bank, a derisory sum of several million dollars. The institute also considers the international account reserves of Canada as a working tool of the Bank of Canada and not to be shared. The position of Bélanger-Campeau is the opposite, that Québec possesses, for all practical purposes, 22% of the assets of the Bank. This amount should be subtracted from the debt to be paid. It is the same for the international reserves. This fundamental disagreement does not augur well for an entente on the common currency!

In the end, there would have to be a compromise. It would cover the public debt of the federal government, the current liabilities, and the partition of assets. One overriding rule applies: the compromise must be politically acceptable to both Québec and Canada.

Table 8

The debt Québec could inherit

($-billion, 1994-95)

	Bélanger-Campeau	Fraser Institute
Financial debt		
Gross debt	546.2	546.2
less Financial assets	40.0	29.2
Adjustments to these assets' value	14.7	—
Equity, crown corporations		5.5
Bills and deposits, Bank of Canada	27.0	
Non-financial assets	79.2	
Subtotal, assets	**160.9**	**34.7**
Net financial debts	385.3	511.5
Québec's share	22.8%	25%
Financial debt allocated to Québec (A)	**87.8**	**127.9**
Other liabilities		
Obligations		
Contracts	—	26.5
Contingent	—	33.0
International	—	16.0
Civial servant pension liabilities	71.0	13.7
Subtotal, other liabilities	71.0	89.2
Québec's share	13.3%	25%
Other liabilities allocated to Québec (B)	**9.5**	**22.3**
Federal assets kept by Québec (C)	**16.4**	**—**
Total debt allocated to Québec (A+B+C)	**113.7**	**150.2**

Sources: Bélanger-Campeau Commission, Fraser Institute

Let's return to the large item: the share of the debt.

The range for percentage share is 22%, 23%, 25%, or even 27%. The difference is important: 2% is equivalent to a debt of $12-billion, or $1700 per Québecer. The extreme criteria are benefits (27%) received and the low 22% proposed by Bélanger-Campeau, the percentage of federal taxes paid from Québec adjusted for certain Ottawa-Québec ententes. The 22% is what Québecers are going to pay if the federal government balances its budget by hiking the taxes of everyone in the same proportion, or if the government of Canada divided the bill of annual deficits among Canadians, according to the taxes that they pay.

Canada would turn down 22% as ridiculously low. It could argue that the debt ought to be reimbursed at the high 27%, according to the benefits received criterion. Examination of federal expenses shows that Québec has received about 27% of Ottawa's expenditures for the past fifteen years, the period over which most of the debt accumulated. "Québec must reimburse for the benefits that it has received and which have not yet been paid," sane Canadians would insist.

Canada would also reject the 22% because it finds its logic in the distribution rule within an integrated Canada. "If you remain, we will apply the distribution formula between rich and poor Canadians. Your percentage will be 22%, thanks to additional effort of the richer provinces. But you reject the Canadian distribution formula when you separate. You cannot win on two counts. So if you remain, you win at 22%. But when you leave you must repay what you received, at 27%."

Canada could also reject 23%, the Québec portion of the Canadian economy. This reflects the capacity to pay. "There is no justification for such a measure," Canada would contend. "Capacity to pay is a criterion that makes sense within a country, because within a country, people agree to share and redistribute income. But between countries, this measuring stick is meaningless."

Twenty-five percent, the demographic weight of Québec, is the compromise of reason. "The marriage is finished. Each takes an equal burden based on its population," the partisans of compromise will assert. In fact, any percentage lower than 25% would likely be politically unacceptable to Canada, obliging the Canadian negotiators to refuse all compromise on the percentage. They would compromise rather on the conditions of repayment, which would also be to Québec's advantage. Thus the partition would probably be 25%.

So what would the total bill be?

We estimate that Québec's bill inherited from Ottawa in separating would lie between $130- and $140-billion. What is more, Québec would probably keep all federal non-financial assets, such as buildings, military bases, airports, on its territory. The secretariat of the Bélanger-Campeau Commission estimated their value at $16-billion.

How could this debt be financed or repaid?

It is on this point that Québec would negotiate fiercely. It would expect concessions from Canada. Contrary to what certain analysts think, a solution would likely be found. Québec could take over its part of the federal debt over a reasonable time period. The two governments could agree to a transfer scaled over five years, permitting the Québec government to refinance the debt on international markets. This refinancing would not be easy, but it is feasible.

But at what rate of interest?

The rate would be higher than the current rate. Consider the average cost of Québec's debt in 1994, about 9%. Interest rates have recently risen as international financial markets have demanded a higher premium for greater risk due to weakness of the Canadian dollar, constitutional uncertainties, and higher debt. The financing rate after separation would also be adjusted for the additional risk due to the increase of the debt. It would constitute one adjustment among others.

This then takes us to the budget of year one in an independent Québec.

13

The Budget in Year One

David Johnston: *In this budget for year one can we focus on the elimination of overlaps and superfluous expenditures, because the elimination of these expenses is an important element in the péquiste strategy to convince Québecers that separation will pay off.*

Marcel Côté: Okay. But first let's consolidate the Québec budget with the budget that we shall take from Ottawa. Then we shall proceed to analyse the potential economies realized in the elimination of duplications and hidden costs. Then let's eliminate superfluous items, particularly in defence. Finally we can establish the fiscal situation of Québec and the amount to be borrowed to cover the deficit, if separation takes place painlessly, and if there were no risk to lenders.

So we start with the consolidation of federal finances.

Table 9 presents the consolidation of our federal "booty," estimated in the previous chapter, with the last provincial budget. The transfers from the federal to the Québec government, $7-billion, are cancelled in the consolidation, being an expense for the federal government and a revenue for the province.

In Table 9 we can also see the relative size of the operational expenses of government where possibilities exist to eliminate duplications. The federal transfer expenditures, which total $15-billion, or 20% of the consolidated budget, do not have overlaps. These are cheques sent to individuals, businesses, and organizations, and not to activities subject to duplication. Interest expenses, defence, education, health, social-service, and income-support expenses offer no possibility of duplication.

In fact, duplications can only exist for certain expenditures that one finds in the category "other operational expenses, provincial and federal." These total $14.3-billion. All these other categories carry no overlaps between the federal and Québec governments. This is not to say compressions are impossible. But these cannot be made in the name of elimination of duplications.

What about the economies to be realized in eliminating these duplications?

The estimates of "doubled up" expenses which could be eliminated vary between $400-million and $3-billion. This last estimate came from Mr. Parizeau during the televised debate in the last provincial election. The Bélanger-Campeau Commission calculated in its report $500-million to $1-billion.

What does one mean by a duplication?

Table 9
Consolidated budget, before adjustments

	$-billion	%
Revenues		
Provincial taxes and other income	28.8	38.0
Federal taxes and other income	26.5	35.0
Total	**55.3**	**73.1**
Program expenditures		
Federal transfers		
to individuals	10.8	14.3
to businesses and organizations	3.3	4.3
to foreigners (CIDA)	0.8	0.1
Subtotal, federal transfers	**14.9**	**19.7**
Education	9.4	12.4
Health and social services	12.8	16.9
Income support	4.3	5.7
Defence (federal)	2.7	3.6
Other provincial operating expenditures	9.7	12.8
Other federal operating expenditures	4.6	6.1
Subtotal, operations	**43.5**	**57.5**
Total, program expenditures	**58.4**	**72.4**
Operating deficit	(3.1)	(4.1)
Debt service		
Provincial component	5.5	7.3
Federal component (9% interest rate)	12.1	16.0
Subtotal	**17.6**	**23.2**
Total expenditures	**75.7**	**100**
Deficit, before cuts	**20.4**	**26.9**

Sources: Federal and Québec budgets, 1994-95

It concerns any activity that is performed by both governments and could be done by one of them with fewer resources than it costs the two. However, remember that duplications are also political balloons dear to politicians. Their elimination offers the illusion of painless reductions in governmental expenses.

But what is the reality?

The studies on this subject describe a complex situation. One conclusion is clear: there is very little duplication in services to the public. For example, the manpower centres of Québec and Ottawa have different mandates and offer different services. The Bureau of Statistics of Québec does not offer the same services as Statistics Canada. In fact, the taxpayer would not tolerate such obvious duplications.

However, duplications exist. Their elimination could translate into savings. Several "doubled up" governmental functions are easy to identify: the National Assembly and the Canadian Parliament, the office of the prime minister in Ottawa and the office of the premier in Québec, Revenue Canada and Revenu-Québec. In several sectors, the two governments do the same thing, in parallel spheres. A common organization, smaller than the sum of the two others, could substitute.

Duplications also exist in support services in the ministries where mandates overlap. For instance, Québec's minister of energy, mines, and forests could undertake functions executed by the federal minister of the same name, engaging to this end federal public servants. But there will be no need to transfer the personnel services functions or the accounting services functions because such services already exist in Québec. Large departments, such as manpower, public works, agriculture, and finance, all present similar savings possibilities. The Québec government would have to hire supplementary personnel for these support functions, but the personnel of the "new" ministry would not equal the sum of the previous two.

How do you calculate the savings that would result from eliminating these duplications?

The number of public servants fairly accurately reflects the level of federal functional expenses. (The defence department is the exception.) We have already arbitrarily assigned 25% of the federal operational expenses to Québec. By extension, we can also assign 25% of the federal public servants before the elimination of duplications. Overlaps will be found only in departments which have a similar mission. This permits us to exclude defence, the RCMP, and the majority of crown corporations, like Canada Post and CN, as well as CBC, an exception to which we shall return later.

If we eliminate defence, the RCMP, and the crown corporations, we are left with some 215,000 federal functionaries in the ministries under consideration and in the agencies that depend on them. Each civil servant represents $80,000 of operational budget.

This is the figure of truth?

Yes, remember this figure: $80,000 of operational budget per civil servant employed. About 140,000 of these public servants work "in the field," outside Ottawa, in regional offices: for example in Canada Manpower Centres and Agriculture Canada's regional offices. In Québec, 33,000 federal functionaries are in the field. After independence these regional offices would be combined with Québec's. There exist very few duplications at the regional and local level, save for office management, unless one cuts the level of services. We estimate that one job out of ten, or 3300, would be eliminated in the field, principally in support functions. The Parti Québécois has committed itself to re-engage all federal public servants "in the field." We should not ignore, however, some exacerbating problems in harmonizing collective agreements.

One also finds 71,000 public servants of these ministries who work in Ottawa-Hull in head office activities. A quarter of them are Québec residents. In the previous chapter we arbitrarily assigned 25% of Ottawa's head office expenses to Québec, as well as 25% of the public servants assigned to these activities, or 18,000 persons. I am assuming that 20% of the federal head office activities are duplicated in Québec. This mainly concerns support activities such as personnel, computers, accounting, research, and so on. In consequence, one federal government job out of five, in Ottawa-Hull, could be eliminated, if the federal responsibilities were consigned to the provinces. This eliminates 3600 public servants in the Ottawa-Hull region. In combining the economies from duplication in the Ottawa area and those in the field, we cut 6900 public servants. At $80,000 per job, the resulting saving is $550-million per year or 12% of the "operational expenses" transferred to Québec.

You have excluded defence, the RCMP, and crown corporations. Could you explain why?

Duplications here are slim because of the uniqueness of these services. CBC is the exception. It "duplicates" Radio-Québec. The French television service of CBC spends $320-million, nearly five times what

Radio-Québec spends. Unless one closes Radio-Québec, the possible economies on rationalization are of the order of $10- to $15-million.

The grand total?

It is $600-million, obtained by the lay-off of some 7500 public servants and CBC employees. A non-recurrent expense on the order of $300-million could also be incurred for the costs of lay-offs. For the purposes of the exercise we have not taken this into account.

Consultants hired by Bélanger-Campeau examined the activities of each federal ministry and concluded that Québec, upon separating, could eliminate 4713 of the 61,237 posts redirected to Québec. Thus their estimate is less than ours. In using the "figure of truth" presented earlier, $80,000 per civil servant, their rationalizations show savings of $377-million, or two-thirds of our estimate.

Other researchers on the Bélanger-Campeau Commission examined different departments to conclude that there could be important savings. Certain analysts have extrapolated these estimates for the whole of government to arrive at eliminations of $1.5-billion. But several weaknesses exist in these extrapolations.

First, the estimates on which they depend are very fragile and hardly viable.

Second, the activities examined by the commission's researchers are not, in their own view, representative.

Finally, one would have to discharge 17,800 public servants in Québec, one out of three, to realize these paper economies. To claim that one federal public servant out of three in Québec does work that could be done by existing Québec personnel without increasing resources stretches credibility.

Our estimate of $600-million should also take into account the losses of economies of scale in Québec, which I think would be minor. The Québec government would have to offer the services that Canada provides to a population four times larger. The necessity of constructing a network of Québec embassies abroad is often cited as an example. But just like duplications, the economies of scale in governmental activities are relatively feeble. Governments generally pay for a level of service proportional to their capacity to pay. Consequently, we have ignored these additional costs in our estimates.

Let's come to an area where there are important rationalizations: national defence and foreign aid.
Canada spends $10.8-billion for national defence. Of that, 46% is for the remuneration of personnel, 29% for expenses of operations (energy, base operations, transport, etc.), and 25% for the acquisition of equipment and parts (airplanes, frigates, helicopters, ammunition). Canada spends $385 per inhabitant, one of the lowest levels in the world. The United States spends $1,000, France $1,100, Sweden $700, and Holland $500. In the current geopolitical context, each industrialized county is called to do its part for world security. In the previous chapter, we kept as the budget of departure, the same level of military expenditures per capita, $385, for a budget on the order of $2.7-billion. The PQ always claims it could reduce military expenses, without stating the amount.

One must realize that Québec cannot act unilaterally to reduce defence spending. Like all other industrialized countries, it must do its share. What is more, the federal government actually spends $2.2-billion in Québec on defence matters, 21% of its budget. Québec has an important military equipment industry. It also wants to maintain military bases in Québec and participate in international alliances, like NATO and NORAD, where one finds Canada and the U.S. Québec would also maintain the Canadian tradition of U.N. peacekeeping operations.

But an independent Québec would face agonizing budget problems. It would certainly cut defence expenses, particularly naval forces. Québecers are less represented in naval personnel, and naval forces are relatively costly. We could keep only a few ships, for the St. Lawrence and the Gulf. We would also keep an air force, reduced but significant. The land forces would be the priority.

We postulate that Québec would cut the military by 25%, or $700-million. This results in a defence budget of $2-billion, or $280 per capita. It's $200-million less than is currently spent in Québec by Ottawa. Québec would rank near the bottom among industrialized countries in defence commitments, a somewhat "egotistical" situation in the current world context. Canada has always felt pressure to maintain its defence expenditures at a level somewhat comparable to its principal geopolitical partners. Québec will experience the same pressures. In the long term it is not certain that Québec could defend itself "on the coattails of others."

Now what about the other instrument of international policy: aid to developing countries?

Canada devotes $115 per capita to foreign aid. Taking account of the difficult circumstances after independence, Québec would try to cut expenditures here. Using our 25% rule, we assigned $800-million to Québec. But the government could not cut that amount significantly.

Table 10
The year-one budget

	$-billion	% of GDP
Revenue (Table 9)	55.3	33.3
Programmes expenditures		
Transfers to individuals	15.1	
Other transfer payments (federal)	3.3	
Education and health	22.2	
Defence and foreign aid	2.7	
Other expenditures	13.7	
Total	**57.0**	**34.3**
Operating deficit	1.7	1.0
Debt service	17.6	10.6
Total expenditures	**74.6**	**44.9**
Year-one deficit, before any cuts and fiscal crisis	**19.3**	**11.6**

Source: Table 9

Why not?

Two reasons. First, Québec must assume international responsibilities. Québecers are perhaps less accustomed to this discourse, because it generally emanates from Ottawa. But as an independent country, Québec cannot escape. A level of $115 (0.6% of GDP) is far from extravagant for an affluent country. Québec will want this instrument principally to retake its influence in the "francophonie" and in multilateral institutions like the World Bank, the Inter American Bank, and the European Bank of Reconstruction and Development.

The second reason is more egotistical. An important part of the money that we give to foreigners is recycled in Canada, under the form of purchases of goods and services. It is a polite secret that Québecers succeed in securing a disproportionately large part of this "CIDA" market. If the Québec government cuts these funds, Québec businesses and Québec NGOs (non-governmental organizations) would be principally affected. They would lobby quite effectively to maintain our engagements in the world.

Nevertheless, we postulate the Québec government could reduce $100-million (12.5%) of its contribution to foreign aid.

Can you summarize this fiscal situation at the beginning of year one?

Table 10 does it. Revenues are $55.3-billion, representing surprisingly only 33.3% of GDP, and reflecting the fact that Québecers do not pay as much in federal taxes as they think. Total expenditures are $73.3-billion. We have taken $1.4-billion out of these expenditures, by eliminating overlaps and reducing defence and foreign aid. Still the deficit is $19.3-billion, nearly 12% of the GDP, even after having eliminated the overlaps!

This number is much higher than what any separatist leaders want to admit. Yet it was relatively easy to calculate, as we have done in the past two chapters, using the official budgets and just adding and subtracting.

Can you summarize the elements of this deficit?

Well, there is another way of arriving at this estimate, and it gives some insight as to why the deficit is so big.

(1) Begin first with the 1994-95 deficit of the Québec government: $5.6-billion.

(2) Add a quarter of the 1994-95 federal deficit, budgeted at $39-billion, or $9.5-billion.

(3) Then add the $3-billion loss on program spending resulting from withdrawing from the Canadian fiscal federal system. As a have-not province, Québec benefits from the redistributive effects of that system.

(4) Add $3-billion to the debt service, for three reasons. Instead of assuming 22% of the national debt, Québecers will now assume 25%. Québec will also pay about 1% more than the federal government on the debt it will patriate. Finally, adding the ongoing liabilities increases the overall debt.

(5) Eliminate overlap and cut defence and foreign aid, to save $1.4-billion.

The total adds to $19.7-billion, a slightly higher estimate than the one obtained by the detailed analysis summarized in Table 10.

Can such a deficit be financed?

Definitely not. But this is not the whole story. Remember the recession caused by the real shocks to the economy, which we investigated in the earlier part of the book. We have not yet factored its impact on the deficit. In fact, the government revenue will be smaller than the one presented in Table 10.

Furthermore, if the government increases taxes and cuts spending, it will have a negative impact on the economy. In other words, the fiscal situation of the Québec government on the day of independence is worse than what Table 10 shows.

There will be a fiscal crisis in Québec if it attempts separation. The numbers just do not add up. The crisis will be terrible.

14

The Fiscal Crisis

David Johnston: *This is a dire prediction, an economic catastrophe! One searches, in vain, for a metaphor capable of capturing your concern. How can this be presented so a layperson can grasp it? And how believable is it?*

Marcel Côté: Simply look to history. What follows is somewhat dry but essential to our understanding.

John Maynard Keynes is the twentieth century's most influential economist. One owes to him the intellectual foundations on which modern macro-economic policies have rested for 50 years. Keynes's major contribution was to identify the forces supporting global demand in the economy. In particular, he isolated the impact of government fiscal policies and monetary policies on the economy, and by ricochet effect, on the level of employment.

Keynes published his principal works during the Great Depression when the fall in private investments caused a collapse of the world economy. Monetary policy was powerless to restart the economy. He recommended a massive increase in governmental spending as the best way to restart the economy.

Today, the teachings of Keynes are totally integrated into our economic thinking. It is difficult to conceive that scarcely 60 years ago, many applauded the original Roosevelt and Mackenzie King cures for the Depression. "The economic crisis will pass with a balanced budget," they said, proposing large cuts in public expenditures. In proposing just the opposite, Keynes gave government the proper tools, allowing it to break the vicious circle of deflation and depression.

Keynes is acutely relevant to Québec's accession to independence. There would be a recession, stemming from the fall of private investments. At the same time, financial markets would constrain the Québec government to reduce expenditures, exactly the contrary to what Keynes prescribed to cure a recession. Unfortunately, Québec would be powerless. The result would convert the separation trauma into a staggering economic crisis.

We understand Keynes's theory. How will this apply in practice?
Let's answer by looking back to ground we have covered. Earlier we referred to the recession caused by the transition shocks to independence. Recall the causes. First, in Montréal we see a significant decrease in economic activity. Second, in the Outaouais, the economic shock would be worse. Third, the agricultural economy will reel from the collapse of the Canadian supply management plan for industrial milk, affecting one-third of the Québec agricultural economy and an important part of the agro-food industry. Exports exceeding $1-billion would evaporate.

The Québec economy simultaneously would be hurt by additional negative impacts. For instance, a ripple effect would transmit the Québec recession into Ontario and the Maritimes. Then this drop in demand would boomerang to strike Québec businesses; 15% of Québec economic output is destined to its neighbours in the east and west. The Québec economy would have to absorb significant price increases as the private sector adapts to new political conditions. Finally, investors would wait to see how the dust settles.

Can you quantify or measure the extent of this crisis?

Even if certain sectors such as natural resources would not be affected much by the political disruptions, this recession would be deep and wide. By way of comparison, in the 1981-82 recession the Québec GDP fell by 3.5%, costing 220,000 workers their jobs. The impact would be greater in an independent Québec. The stabilizing effects of Canadian fiscal federalism would also be lost. When there is a recession in the east of the country, as will be the case, the west continues to pay duties and taxes. This money "flows" towards the regions in recession. This stabilizing effect is an important contribution of federalism to absorb recessionary impact. In leaving the Canadian fiscal system, Québec loses these automatic stabilizers. Recessions, under post-separation conditions, would always be harsher than current recessions.

And the impact on the Québec government?

The budget revenues of year one were calculated without taking this recession into account. As out fiscal system is progressive, the impact of recessions on government finances is always more pronounced than the impact on the general economy. Let us assume the recession causes economic production to fall by 3%, which is a minimum. The result would be revenue reductions of $1.5- to $2-billion, and expenditure increases of $0.5- to $1-billion, because of the unemployment and welfare increases, for a $2- to $3-billion increase in the deficit. This supplementary spike would put the deficit of the Québec government over the $20-billion mark, a mind-boggling deficit that would scare any finance minister making deficit projections for an independent Québec.

Could such a deficit be financed? What is the borrowing capacity of an independent Québec?
The borrowing capacity of a government is principally determined by international credit agencies, such as Standard and Poor's and Moody's, and by Canadian counterparts, such as Canadian Bond Rating Services. These agencies will be astonished by the financial situation of the Québec government. Indeed, this situation will be unique.

Can you explain further?
The Québec financial situation will present a combination of four relatively unusual, or should I say, extreme conditions.

First, the high level of indebtedness, putting Québec in the same league as the worst countries in the world in this respect, such as Italy, Greece, and Belgium. Government debt would total 125% of GDP, a very high figure. The total public debt issued or guaranteed by the public sector would be close to 160% of GDP, probably a world record. These would be the first unusual "warts."

The second problem: the fact that a significant portion of this debt would be held by foreigners, nearly $120-billion. That's a lot of money!

Even the worst debtor countries in the world, such as Italy and Greece, finance their debt mostly domestically. Québec would owe too much to non-Québecers. The payments of interest on that debt would be a terrible drain on its balance of payments.

Thirdly, the budgetary deficit. We estimated above that just by adding numbers found in today's federal and Québec budgets and factoring in a recession, the deficit would be above $22-billion, a whopping 13% of GDP. That would not happen! The government would not be able to borrow it. But let us say that whatever the final number is, the deficit will be high, too high for the taste of the credit agencies.

Finally, there would be this unusual arrangement with the government of Canada, covering $135-billion of debt. The arrangement would probably say that this debt will be transferred to Québec as soon as it can pick it up on its own. But $135-billion for a small country; that has never been seen.

I bet the credit agencies' reports on Québec are likely to be among the thickest and most complex ever written. But their conclusion is likely to be simple: Don't touch Québec unless something drastic is done to reduce indebtedness.

Can we quantify the situation of the Québec government?

Sure. Look at the table following. It is based on numbers coming out before any deficit reduction adjustment. I also took out the effects of the recession, to make the calculations easier.

The first two of the four columns present actual statistics for the federal government and the Québec government. The third column presents the statistics as if the Québec government and the Canadian government were now a single payer: the numbers are consolidated. The last column belongs to the government of a separate Québec. By comparing it with the other ones, you can see how Québec's financial picture deteriorates with separation.

Can you take us through some of these figures?
Let us look at the figures in the "Québec alone" column that will scare the financial community. First, government expenditures, 49.9% of GDP and, more importantly, nearly 7% more than the consolidated total. This high level of spending is due to the loss of efficiency and to the high debt service charges faced by the government. The table assumes the government is offering the same level of service as the combined federal-provincial levels do now. This is one thing that would not last.

Table 11
Québec credit rating

	Canada federal	Québec prov.	Qué.-Can. consolidated	Québec alone
	(base 1994-95)			
Revenue/GDP	17.1	21.7	34.4	33.3
Expenditures/GDP	22.6	25.1	43.3	49.9
Deficit/GDP	5.5	3.4	8.9	11.6
Interest expenses/revenues	36.4	19.1	n.a.	31.8
Direct gross debt/GDP	76.4	39.6	116.0	120.9
Public debt/GDP	125.0	77.1	153.5	158.4
Foreign debt/GDP	25.6	40.2	n.a.	72.0

Sources: Statistics Canada, Department of Finance, Québec and Canada, Tables 9 and 10

Secondly, the deficit, which is 11.6% of the GDP. Remember, I have not factored in any recession. Nevertheless, this is still too high by world standards.

Thirdly, the direct debt of the government, 121% of GDP, and the total public sector debt, 158.4% of GDP, which put Québec in the same class as Italy. But we part with Italy on the fourth point, the debt held by foreigners, $120-billion, or 72% of GDP.

This is the astounding figure. Some of this is due to the debt owed to Canada, which I estimate at $55- to $60-billion. The rest is to Americans, Europeans, and Japanese. The problem with such a high level of foreign debt is that it cannot be solved easily, quickly. There is nobody left in the world with the resources or will to pick up the debt. Foreigners are likely to say, enough is enough.

Finally, the last number. Have you noticed anything unusual in that table? Look carefully at the revenue number in an independent Québec: 33.3% of GDP, a low number for a basket case. Every lender will jump at seeing that number. You and I have to get ready if Québec ever separates. That number is bound to increase. Do your share, the lenders will say. Tax, tax, tax, that's what they will say.

Don't we pay high taxes in Québec?

Yes and no. Yes, given our ability to pay, but no, compared with the share paid in most other industrialized countries. Thirty-three percent is the actual share of Québec GDP taken by the two levels of government from the taxpayers' pockets, a number smaller than in Ontario. This is one of the things masked by our federal system. The statistics would be even lower for the Atlantic provinces and for Manitoba and

Saskatchewan. Our tax system is progressive — rich people pay more taxes than ordinary people. What that number says is that there are fewer rich people in Québec than commonly thought, so the average rate of taxation is lower.

One thing is definite. Taxpayers in an independent Québec will be hit by tax hikes, significant tax hikes. Lenders are not fools.

Have credit agencies said anything on this?

Not much so far. You see, credit agencies are in business. They are paid by borrowers to evaluate their debt issues. Keep that in mind; borrowers pay to have their creditworthiness assessed. Nobody has asked the agencies or paid them to assess the creditworthiness of an independent Québec. And I will bet that the agencies will keep their mouths shut. It's all hypothetical, they will say. They avoid controversy like plague. They already have enough of it.

But anybody can tell that with such numbers, Québec debt will be assessed as being sub-investment grade, a low B at most. Credit agencies give A's and B's to debt issue. The A's are further broken down into AAA, AA, and A, and so are the B's. Furthermore, some agencies add "plus" and "minus" to these A's and B's. So this is a fine-toothed rating system. But there is a threshold level, between A and B. Most pension funds and insurance companies, which are the biggest buyers of bonds, are limited in the percentage of B debt they can buy. So because there are so few buyers, there is not much of a market for B-rated debt.

Québec is now single A, the lowest A. Taking into account the numbers shown in the table, separation would put us at the low-B level, or we would probably be ungraded. Simple as that.

What would that mean?

Big problems. Québec now borrows about $7-billion a year, including the refinancing of debt arriving at maturity. About 55% of that borrowing is done abroad. Its financial situation is well known. It would be even better known the day after separation.

Lenders are somewhat stuck with borrowers, an odd couple. So they cannot walk away from Québec if they want to be repaid the $200-billion debt. Their bargaining tool is new money, financing the ongoing deficit. So the question is: What will borrowers do?

This is hard to say at the moment, but all the ingredients are there to constitute a major world finance crisis. To say the least, Québec's total public indebtedness, $200-billion, is big money. Here is a scenario. The international lenders would band together and work with the G-7 governments and the International Monetary Fund, like they did when the USSR broke up and its old debt was apportioned. They would first demand that Québec significantly reduce its deficit. Let us assume for a moment that they would demand that Québec reduce its current deficit to $12-billion. From over $22-billion to $12-billion. That is a significant reduction. After all, $12-billion is still a big number, over 7% of the GDP.

By the way, it is also the number that many economists in Québec have said that the government of a separate Québec could finance.

Could Québec do that?

This is where Mr. Keynes comes into the picture. That is most ironic. Jacques Parizeau is a disciple of Keynes. He studied economics in England and shares Keynes's theory about the important role that the government must play to sustain the level of economic activity, particularly in hard times when real shocks slow the economy down. Keynes would be saying to Jacques: "Separating is tough for the economy. Private demand will fall. You have to expand government spending."

But lenders would be saying just the opposite: "Forget Keynes and reduce that deficit by $10-billion." Keynes says that if a government does that, it will deflate the economy. But taking money out of the economy, it drags the economy down.

Mr. Parizeau will be caught between the hard-nosed lenders and Mr. Keynes. The lenders will win. But here is where it really hurts. The combination of tax hikes and spending cuts to achieve that $10-billion reduction of the deficit is much bigger than $10-billion, as Keynes has taught us.

If the government of Québec cuts its expenses by $10-billion, or augments its taxes to cover a portion, the Keynesian effect comes into play. When the government lowers its expenditures, it deflates the economy in the same breath. Its revenues from taxes will diminish proportionally. Jacques Parizeau, a professor of economics, knows about the Keynesian effect.

Some years ago, John McCallum and Chris Green, McGill University economists, calculated the Keynesian effect for the economy of a separate Québec:

- One dollar of expenditure reduction translates into a 57-cent reduction in the deficit.
- One dollar of tax increases translates into a 62-cent reduction in the deficit.

If a marginal rate of efficiency of 60% is used, the deficit reduction from $22-billion to $12-billion would require a combination of cuts and tax increases of $18-billion, or 20% of the budget! This is politically impossible. A deflationary spiral leads the economy into a deeper and deeper stagnation, while the government searches for resources that it progressively squeezes. Such cuts would rapidly create a social and political crisis without precedent, while a major depression relentlessly takes form. Québec might have to declare bankruptcy on its debt, but would also be incapable of borrowing to meet its operational budget.

Could such a crisis really come about?

We have just observed it in certain countries of the former Soviet Union, and notably in Russia. But in Québec, we are in a state of denial.

When such nightmares emerge, the International Monetary Fund generally intervenes, replacing the financial markets that refuse to lend. The IMF is used to bearing the blame. Wherever it is called to intervene with a "restructuring" program, the IMF leaves a bitter memory. It would make demands that would astonish Québecers, indeed shock them, such as insisting they sell Hydro-Québec, most likely to foreigners. Québecers won't believe it. But it is clear that Hydro-Québec would be at the top of the IMF list.

Nevertheless, the other countries in which the IMF has intervened have an advantage on Québec. They had their own currency. But the Parti Québécois affirms that it would forego this benefit.

Well then, let us peer inside the fiscal crisis for a moment, to examine what would happen to currency in Québec.

15

Québec's Financial Needs

David Johnston: *Can you cite precedents of fiscal crises to guide us?*

Marcel Côté: Yes, a recent one, in Sweden. It all started in early September 1992, in Finland, which was seized with an economic crisis and devalued its currency immediately. In the same week the crisis spread to Sweden, Finland's neighbour and its second largest commercial partner. With 8.3 million inhabitants, a little more than Québec, Sweden is one of the world's richest countries. Its standard of living is similar to ours. But Sweden also borrows abroad, and its government was also beset with a major structural deficit.

As soon as the currency crisis struck in Finland, analysts predicted that Sweden could no longer avoid a devaluation. Too many negative factors besieged Sweden: Finnish currency devaluation; Russian economic crisis; Swedish government budget deficit; balance of payments deficit; and finally, inflation. The Swedish economy was in bad shape. The analysts were unanimous: the crisis was inevitable. All that was missing was a catalyzing element, until Finnish devaluation. That tipped the balance.

In the weeks following, the Bank of Sweden resisted, clearly affirming its intention not to devalue the crown. It would go right to the limit. No question of devaluation. The unconditional support of the government of Sweden was taken for granted. But the message of the monetary authorities was disbelieved — by millions of Swedes.

What did they do?

They sent their savings to shelter in the storm. They rushed to the telephone to order their bankers to sell their Swedish crowns — to buy American dollars or German marks. On one Friday, $4.5-billion took wing — in eight hours, one of the largest flights of funds ever observed. Swedish authorities couldn't believe their eyes. "What's happened to us? What's happened to Sweden?"

Four and a half billion dollars is perhaps only 2% of Sweden's GDP. But it is also 75% of the Bank of Sweden's reserves. All this flew the country in eight hours. Neither bank nor government could stop telephone transfers. The monetary authorities had recourse to all modern means to arrest the flight of capital. On the Friday night, the Bank of Sweden hiked its interest rate. But nothing could stop the sudden migration. "What will happen to us?" demanded the Swedes. That weekend many Swedes cancelled their regular visits to the country.

The battle lasted several weeks. Interest rates were raised incredibly high, to keep money in the country. One weekend they were pushed up to 500% (yes, 500%). The cabinet was reshuffled. Major spending cuts were announced. Taxes were increased.

To no avail. In November, the Bank of Sweden gave up. Money

continued to flee. The manoeuvre failed. The Swedish government abandoned its course. It devalued the Swedish crown by 15%. Like quicksilver, financial markets stabilized. Slowly the Swedes brought their money back into the country. The result: People 1, Government 0.

What lessons can we learn from Sweden?

The Swedish monetary crisis is an example of the fragility of undisciplined economies who abuse debt and deficits. The more people have savings, the greater the vulnerability. Governments no longer control these savings. The Swedish crisis is a good example of the limits of governments, even the most powerful, forcing their citizens to swallow a dose of monetary medicine in periods of peril and confiscating their savings. Consider France and Mr. Mitterrand in 1982. The French became anxious with his socialism. Money began to leave the country. Mr. Mitterrand accepted his fate. The franc was devalued. Socialist policies were trashed. Great Britain and Mrs. Thatcher experienced a similar fate in 1992.

One new and overwhelming element. We live in the age of electronic currency. When economic storms rise, people who are substantial savers put their savings into shelter — electronically. The stratagem is simple: significant sums of domestic savings are converted into foreign currencies, until the storm passes. The operation is done rapidly, in the space of several days at most. And for individual transactions, seconds.

For the majority of Swedes, the crisis of 1992 was a house of cards. It collapsed, without warning. A small part of the population succeeded in protecting the value of its savings. The large majority — made up of many, many small savers — was the loser. In the days that followed, the Swedish parliament, convened in emergency, imposed an emergency plan, cutting social expenditures and hiking taxes. Sweden's lesson is telling for independent Québec. Québec is in bad financial form now, with government deficits and public debt. It would be less in shape after independence.

Québec also depends heavily on foreign borrowing. By contrast, Québecers have substantial personal savings. They will want to shelter these during the storm. Will Québecers act differently from the Swedes of 1992? Or the French of 1982? Could there be a monetary crisis associated with independence?

Can you put in place the pieces of the puzzle that could produce a monetary crisis and explain what it means?
At the same time that our governments are "broke," many individual Québecers have substantial savings. Table 12 shows the balance sheet of Québec households, as we can infer from a 1992 Bank of Canada study and on data on bank deposits and loans in Québec. A balance sheet presents in summary form at one moment in time financial assets and liabilities. On the plus side this includes their deposits at the bank and Caisses populaires, portfolios of stocks and bonds, and pension funds. We can also add the value of their fixed assets, such as houses and cars. On the minus side this includes personal debts, such as mortgages and personal loans. The results are surprising. The balance sheet is largely positive.

One can still speak of Québecers' indebtedness. But it is their governments that are indebted, not they themselves. The balance sheet of individual Québecers is very healthy, resting on solid savings showing a net worth on the order of $300-billion. Obviously, peoples' ages play key roles. People 45 and older have more positive balance sheets. They've had time to accumulate wealth. Wealth is also more concentrated than income. People with higher incomes and older than 45 hold an important part of these assets. But they constitute a small proportion of the population.

The table also indicates that a substantial part of these assets is liquid, meaning readily convertible to cash. Seventy billion dollars is on deposit in Québec banks and credit unions. Although significant amounts are placed for a term, these deposits can be very mobile. In case of crisis, depositors can lift a part of the $75-billion and place it elsewhere. A simple telephone call suffices. But it goes without saying that these deposits don't sleep in the banks and the credit unions. They have been placed out in the form of mortgage loans, business loans, bond purchases, and so on. In fact, net assets (what is left after deposits have been lent out) of the banking system represent only 5% of its balance sheet. The balance sheet of banking institutions in Québec is $120-billion. This represents net assets in the system of $6-billion, roughly equal to their liquid or cashable reserves. This amount is minimal compared with Québecers' deposits of $71-billion.

Table 12
Québec households balance sheet (1994)

Deposits, banks and caisses	71	Mortgages	55
Other deposits	4	Other loans	36
Bonds	18	**Total, debt**	**91**
Equity	47		
Life insurance and pensions	63	Net worth	282
Subtotal, financial assets	**203**		
Non-financial assets	170		
Total	**373**		

Sources: Statistics Canada, Bank of Canada, Mouvement Desjardins

Let us introduce here a key Québec financial institution, the pension fund manager called the Caisse de dépôt et de placement. Québec politicians speak often of the Caisse as a national treasure. The Caisse de dépôt, true to its name, receives deposits, that is, monies collected for diverse pension funds controlled by the government, and reserve funds from the public agencies handling automobile and health insurance, and so on. As of December 31, 1993, the Caisse managed assets of $47-billion, as Table 13 shows. As its full name also suggests, these monies are outplaced promptly. The Québec government and its agencies are the principal beneficiaries. The Caisse favours the purchase of their bonds, which represent 37% of its assets. About $2-billion of Caisse funds are placed outside Québec, principally in liquid investments.

Table 13
Balance sheet of the Caisse de dépôt et de placement
December 31, 1993 ($-billion)

Deposits (Liabilities)		Investments (Assets)	
Québec Pension Plan	16.4	Québec government debt	17.4
Other pension funds	20.3	Other fixed income debt	7.9
Insurances reserves	10.0	Equities	17.8
Others	.4	Mortgages and real estate	3.6
		Other assets	.4
Total	**47.1**	**Total**	**47.1**

Source: Caisse de dépôt et de placement

The Caisse is a large institution. But all its money is invested. In case of crisis the government cannot count on the Caisse for more than a few billion dollars quickly available. The Caisse would first have to sell some assets to liberate any funds. Ninety percent of these funds are invested in Québec. To sell these investments would only aggravate the crisis. Thus the Caisse could free up some funds, but relatively few in comparison with the $71-billion that Québecers hold in their bank accounts.

Many Québecers misunderstand the true role of the Caisse. It is not a banker that must continually ensure the liquidity of its deposits. Rather, the Caisse receives funds to invest for the long term. Thus it cannot turn them over quickly. The Caisse is a giant. But this giant moves very slowly. In crisis it would be of little use. Its funds are already fully invested.

What role would foreign loans play in all this?

We count on them. All governments in Canada now are heavily dependent on foreign lenders. The Québec government has borrowed $22-billion, Hydro-Québec, $27-billion, and other Québec government institutions, $7-billion, for a total of $56-billion of public foreign loans. Other provinces are nearly as dependent. There is $100-billion of federal debt held by foreigners. This is the degree of our dependence on foreigners, nearly $300-billion for Canada as a whole.

After independence, the Québec government and its agencies would owe about $110-billion, or nearly $15,000 per inhabitant, to non-Québecers. No people in the world would be so dependent on public loans from abroad. Other countries, like Italy, or other provinces, like Newfoundland, are now more indebted than Québec. But no jurisdiction is as indebted to foreigners as Québec would be. The Québec government would be the world champion.

By contrast, Québec-based businesses depend relatively little on foreigners to finance themselves — several billion dollars at the most. Even investments in Québec by foreign-owned investors, like IBM, General Motors, Iron Ore, Pechiney, probably do not exceed $20-billion.

And Québec financial institutions?
They are intermediaries.

What does this mean? Are they creditors or debtors facing the world?
Available statistics are not sufficient to make a definitive estimate. But it is quite probable that they are net debtors borrowing more than they invest abroad. According to Bank of Canada statistics, Canadian chartered banks lend about $5-billion more in Québec than they take as deposits. In fact, as a "neutral" intermediary, the financial system is adapted to the real Québec balance sheet. Thus, each year, Québec borrows more from foreigners than it invests. Government is the principal borrower, but the rest of the economy is also a net debtor.

This leads us then to the net money in or net money out position, or the current account balance of Québec.
Yes. If you take the whole of revenues paid to Québec from outside and subtract the whole of the expenditures made by Québec outside, you obtain the current account balance. It can be in surplus or in deficit. If the whole Québec economy were to earn more abroad than it spent, there would be a surplus, and a net saving. If the whole of

Québec were to spend collectively more than it earned, there would be a deficit; the whole of Québec must then borrow from outside to meet the deficit. These borrowings take place directly, when the government borrows from abroad, or indirectly, via the financial system, when individuals and businesses borrow from the banks; the banks, as intermediaries, finance these loans with deposits which come from outside Québec.

In practice the balance of the current account is not measured in adding the revenues and the expenditures of *all* the participants in the economy. This would be too complicated and imprecise. Rather one uses an easier measure, the transactions Québecers do with foreigners: the exports and imports of products, service transactions such as tourism and insurance, payments and gifts from governments and relatives, and interest and dividend payments involving foreigners. In all of these cases, there will be some Québecers who receive and others who give. The total of these additions and subtractions give the current account balance.

Current account balance is one measure international financiers follow most keenly in evaluating investment risk in a country. If the balance is positive, the country saves and invests abroad. This is a good risk sign. If the balance is negative, the country is indebted more and more each year to foreigners. More vigilance is necessary.

Table 14 presents for 1994 the current account balance for Canada, and for Québec as if it were an independent country. This latter case is an estimate. We do not have official statistics on the external exchanges of Québec, in particular the exchanges with the rest of Canada. But we can estimate the value of Québec exports and imports of goods, in services, and payments of net interest and dividends to non-Québecers.

Table 14
The current account deficit

(1993, $-billion)

	Canada		Separate Québec	
	$	% GDP	$	% GDP
Exports	181.3	26.4	66.4	40%
Imports	171.8	25.0	66.4	40%
Trade balance	9.5	1.4	0	0
Services, net balance	-13.8	-2.0	-4.3	-2.6%
Dividends, interests, transfers,net	-26.4	-3.8	-9.3	-5.6%
Current account deficit	-30.7	-4.5	-13.6	-8.2%

Source: Review of the Bank of Canada

The Canadian situation will not surprise anyone. The statistics are regularly published. The Canadian deficit is disquieting. Its cause is known. This is principally interest paid to foreigners for government loans and dividends on direct investments in Canadian businesses.

The negative balance of the Québec current account is less well known. There are no official statistics on this subject. However, one knows that Québec has a slight surplus in its trade balance, exports less imports. The trade surplus is not as large as Canada's, but it is generally positive. Just like Canada, Québec has an important deficit in services. Tourism is the principal culprit. So long as it is warm and beautiful in the south during the winter, we will have a deficit, the attraction of snow being insufficient to replace all the money spent south, in Florida, in particular.

Separation would worsen by about $3-billion the combined deficit on trade and services. This is the amount of net federal transfers

Québec would lose under separation and which would show up as a negative in the current account.

What about interest?

This is where separation would bring about major changes. Québec's debt to foreigners would increase dramatically, and so would its debt services. For instance, Québecers own only about $80-billion in federal debt. But they would inherit, if our calculations are right, $135-billion. This represents $55-billion of additional foreign debt. In fact it is only $44-billion of new foreign debt, from a balance of payments perspective, because 20% of Ottawa's debt is already owned by foreigners. But the annual debt service on that $44-billion additional debt is $4-billion, which goes straight into the current account. As a result, the overall deficit, before any correction sets in, is a whopping $13.6-billion, or 8% of GDP. This is the level of deficit that Mexico had in late 1994 when the peso crisis erupted. It simply is not sustainable. It is a level rarely observed around the world.

At the opposite extreme, Japan records a surplus equal to 3% of its GDP. The European Union in the stated rules for convergence to establish a common currency used 3% as the maximum. A country cannot join the monetary union without meeting this condition. A larger deficit imposes financial operations too big to be supported by the common financial system. If Québec becomes independent, this statistic will be dramatized in financial circles. They will conclude, as will the majority of economists, that this is unsustainable.

So what would Québec have to do?

Simple. Devalue its currency, the only remedy able to produce the profound adjustments required for a major correction on the current account. Look at Mexico in Christmas week 1994.

Can you now show us the financial position of independent Québec on "D Day" when this crisis would be likely to happen?
The following figure features the principal actors in the financial drama of Québec on its first day of independence. Québec citizens are the first players with a positive balance, financial assets of $200-billion, about half of which are liquid or cashable, and debts of $90-billion. The Québec government (including Hydro-Québec), a second great player, would have liabilities of $200-billion, of which at least $80-billion would be owed to foreigners, including Canada. This is an actor with a $20- to $25-billion deficit, and the requirement to make cuts. In the wings we find the Caisse de dépôt with $40-billion of assets but only $2- or $3-billion, liquid.

The financial institutions of Québec are intermediaries with net assets of only $6- to $7-billion. They have received $120-billion from one group and have lent this to another. Not surprising that these institutions yearn for stability.

What is your fundamental message?
Examine the following figure carefully. These are the critical financial players on D Day. The balance sheet of individual Québecers is important and healthy. But they are nervous. Increasingly so. Foreign lenders realize that Québec has become the world champion of borrowers following the consolidation of federal loans with those of Québec. They are also nervous. At last, watch zealously the *dramatis personae* of the Québec government with its debt of $200-billion, its

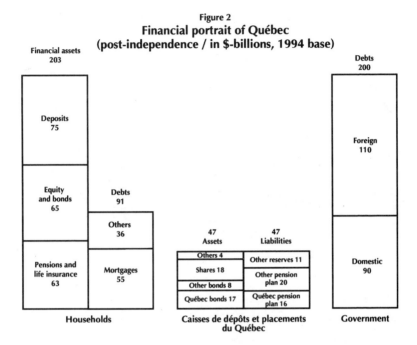

Figure 2
Financial portrait of Québec
(post-independence / in $-billions, 1994 base)

budget deficit of $15- to $20-billion after harsh cuts and a deficit on its current account of 8% of GDP. This player wants independence, freedom, room to breathe, run, and celebrate. Remember Paul and Virginia about to run the marathon.

16

The Monetary Crisis

David Johnston: *But we have now started the marathon. What do the first few metres show?*

Marcel Côté: Québec's financial statements on D Day, as shown above, are not considered yet by the financial markets, which do not now anticipate the independence of Québec. The marathon has not yet begun. That is why, at the moment when these lines are written, the Québec government only pays an interest premium of 1% on its borrowing in relation to the government of Canada. But these things can change dramatically at the sound of the gun, and even before. As Québec approaches D Day, and if markets sense the Québec people support separation.

Doesn't this suggest that international financial markets do not have a lot to say on the question of independence?

Strictly speaking, no. If Québecers want independence, then Québec could become independent, as far as markets are concerned. The great majority of the millions of investors who feed the international financial markets would respect the choice of Québecers. They would not shed any tears over the end of Canada as we know it today. Financial markets lack sentiment. As long as you do not ask for money.

Financial markets do concern themselves with Québec's credit and the monetary arrangements that would result. They may lack sentiment, but they are not indifferent, so long as their money is at stake. Never forget: Québec will be a very important international borrower. Then they will have a great deal to say on the costs of independence.

All right, let us look at what could happen in the months or even years preceding D Day, while the Canadian and Québec negotiators look for compromises in the very complex divorce proceedings between Québec and Canada.

We begin with a very restrictive monetary policy. It is not only Québec which is not in good financial condition. Canada is not for the same reasons: excessive indebtedness of governments and an inability to constrain deficits within reasonable limits. For several years, the International Monetary Fund has warned Canada: There is a limit to indebtedness.

There are healthy aspects to the Canadian economy that somewhat compensate for government abuses. In 1994 and 1995 economic growth in Canada will probably lead the industrialized world. The financial balance sheet of Canadian households is even better than that of Québecers. But as I've been saying, government debt and deficit are deeply disturbing.

Okay, let's accept the hypothesis that the referendum is won

and, miraculously, that the rest of Canada has succeeded in agreeing with Québec on a mandate to negotiate and has confided this to a federal-provincial team. Let's also accept the hypothesis that the negotiations conclude with an agreement. The political debate requires that the highly improbable also be analysed. So, what happens?

The Canadian public sector has one of the largest deficits of the industrialized countries. Lenders are far from enchanted with divorce. Put yourself in the shoes of a lender who learns, without its advice being sought, that in several months the mortgage it holds on a duplex will be divided in two, one for the upper apartment, the other for the lower apartment.

Lenders will then try to distance themselves from Canadian government bonds and treasury bills. But the governments must continue to borrow. In fact, giving the short-term maturity of half of Canadian debt, there is about $300-billion of government debt that must be financed each year in Canada. These are government bonds and treasury bills whose term has expired and must be repaid or rolled over — that is, refinanced. That's a lot to digest in the middle of a divorce.

The Bank of Canada will try to help the governments. To prevent the house of debt cards from crashing, it will raise interest rates. Normally there is nothing like a rise in interest rates to calm uncertainty. In fact, the Bank of Canada has already tightened the monetary reins in Canada. Canadian interest rates are much higher than those of the United States due to our problems. During the increasing period of uncertainty paralleling the divorce negotiations, the attention of politicians would be fixed on share of the booty, and not on reduction of the debt. The Bank of Canada would be obliged to hike the interest rate further to make investment in the Canadian debt more attractive.

The entire Canadian economy would suffer from a tightening of conditions, as it did in 1990-91, when credit tightening worsened the recession. This would happen at a bad moment. And it is just what business does not want. When uncertainty grows and the economy slows in anticipation of Québec separation, the Bank of Canada would raise interest rates, thus further discouraging investment by business. This is the vicious circle of a perilously indebted country. While a generous monetary policy is a welcome elixir for the economy, public indebtedness requires restrictiveness. It is just as if Paul and Virginia began their marathon with shoes a size or two too small. Not only are they in poor condition; they are badly equipped.

This is what would happen before separation. Can you summarize the peril?

A triple calamity would strike a Québec embarking for the promised land. First there would be the real shocks to the economy, which would start to be felt, led by the torpedoes referred to earlier. Secondly, the government of Québec would be obliged to follow a deflationary fiscal policy, cutting its expenses by several billion dollars to lower its borrowing needs dramatically, as it prepared for separation. Thirdly, the Bank of Canada monetary policy would be very restrictive, to prevent the mountain of Canadian public debts from crashing down. Totally the opposite of what is prescribed. This policy would only worsen things.

Must it be the captive?

As long as it is in Canada, yes. After separation — that is another story.

Some economists and university professors have emphasized that it would be possible for Québec to use the Canadian dollar after independence. It would be difficult for Canada to prevent it from doing so. The indépendantiste leaders, for their part, have emphasized that their preferred option is to use the Canadian dollar. The experts' position, defensible in theory, is, however, incomplete.

The real question is not to know if the Canadian dollar could be used in an independent Québec. Because in theory, the answer is yes, just as the American dollar could be used as the official currency of Canada. The question is twofold: whether the Canadian dollar would actually be used in an independent Québec and how much such a monetary system would last. It is not the government alone which decides what currency is used; the users of the currency have a say, too.

One can understand why the indépendantiste leaders prefer the Canadian dollar in an independent Québec. There would already be enough uncertainty in the air, and they have no desire to add anxieties connected to a new currency of unknown value. Québecers are attached to the Canadian dollar, for legitimate reasons. All their savings are in this currency. Contracts of employment, insurance policies, pension regime arrangements, all these are written in Canadian dollars. All these engagements could be thrown into question by the introduction of a new currency. Québecers would also lack confidence in the value of a Québec dollar, which would be forcibly devalued and would lose its purchasing power. The new indépendantiste regime would face enough problems with independence. It would neither need nor want these additional problems of confidence. What is more, it is not certain that many Québecers would opt for independence if they knew that they would be left with a Québec currency of uncertain value.

The Bank of Canada would probably not oppose the Québec government's use of the Canadian dollar as legal currency. A service agreement giving Québec institutions access to the Canadian Payments Association, where every night cheques from all banks are cleared, would be required. The Bank of Canada would further require a formal segregation by country of the balance sheet of financial institutions operating in the two countries and the maintenance of distinct reserves. Thus, each of the Big Five chartered banks would form a Québec subsidiary. This segregation would assure that the Canadian assets and liabilities of institutions operating in Canada regulated by the bank are clearly separated from the Québec assets and liabilities. Otherwise, it would be necessary for the Bank of Canada to regulate, for example, the Mouvement Desjardins, which it does not do now.

Can you explain this in more detail and why?

The Canadian chartered banks would maintain distinct reserves for their Québec subsidiaries, and vice versa for the Banque Nationale. The latter would carry on business in Canada with a subsidiary of its own. It would separate its accounts and dedicate to them either exclusive Canadian or Québec reserves. Banks understand these regulations as they already apply to our foreign subsidiaries. It is normal practice for institutions carrying on business in more than one country to segregate their reserves.

So where's the rub?

In Québec's case this policy would have an important impact. Many financial analysts would predict that this entente for Québec to use the Canadian currency would not last long. Thus it is essential that the two systems be separated. In segregating balance sheets, Canada would immunize itself against banking crises in Québec. But it would be more difficult for the Québec government to counter a bank crisis in Québec.

But what leads these analysts to anticipate the breakdown of this system — a banking crisis?

Let us return to the balance of current accounts discussed in Chapter 15. An independent Québec economy would show an excessive deficit in its current account balance. The deficit may not be as high as the 8% of GDP indicated in Chapter 15 as the Québec economy would plunge into profound recession, depressing imports and reducing the deficit on the current account. Nevertheless, Québec as a whole would borrow a significant share of its GDP annually to pay the excess of expenditures over its revenues. These borrowings would be made directly by the sale of government bonds abroad, or by the banking system as an intermediary. But there are limits to these loans. In particular, the Québec banking system would be required to renew its liquidity reserves, which only represent 2% to 3% of GDP, with foreign borrowings. The banking system would hesitate to put itself "in the red" in Québec. Some of the best experts in monetary matters are found in banks. These experts well understand that the Québec economy does not satisfy the criteria of convergence to share a currency with Canada. They would signal to their bosses that the common Québec-Canada currency would not have a long life. Prudence would dictate that they avoid excessive loans to maintain their liquidities in Québec.

They would not be alone in arriving at these conclusions. Many very creditable economists affirm today that a common currency is unsustainable, for the same reasons. The Québec economy has a current account deficit much too high to "converge" with that of Canada and thus to share the same currency. The high borrowings of the Québec government, over 10% of GDP during accession to independence, more than half of it obtained from abroad, would bring about too much instability. The Québec recession, much harsher than elsewhere in Canada, would increase this instability. The monetary entente could not last, they would advise their clients.

And who are the key actors?

These clients are, in general, the financial institutions and the large individual savers. A great number already do not favour independence. Remember the illustration of quickfooted savings in the previous chapter. The wealth which figures in the Québec balance sheet is not equally distributed. The more fortunate classes principally hold this wealth. Among the households with most positive balance sheets, we find an over-representation of people 45 years or older, persons with higher incomes, and anglophones — populations where support for independence is feeblest.

These people will want to shelter at least a part of their savings from the breakup of the common currency. Telephone calls by 25%

of Québec savers instructing their bankers to transfer part of their savings into non-Québec accounts would suffice. An amount greater than all the bank reserves could leave Québec. The banks would have to decide whether to borrow from abroad to reconstitute these reserves.

What else could they do?

Monetary history teaches us what financial institutions do when there is a massive flight of capital. They try to accommodate their savers while limiting their own risk. Their solutions to maintain their reserves is to restrain credit. They cut back on loans. The countries of Eastern Europe, Slovakia, and the Ukraine have just shown it.

What happens then?

Within a few days the banking system would impose a tough tightening of liquidity. What follows next is expected: loans are called; accounts are emptied to reimburse these loans; liquidity in the system stiffens. One forgets sometimes that banking systems function on small margins of capital (4% of deposits) and of liquidity (7% of their assets in readily cashable treasury bills and Bank of Canada deposits). These reserves are sufficient when people have confidence in the banking system. If a single bank is in crisis, deposits which leave that bank find their way back into other banks. The system remains in equilibrium. But during an accession to independence we would have a crisis of confidence that would strike the entire Québec banking system. Deposits would quit the Québec system. Too many experts doubt that a common currency would last for long. The Québec banking system would be at peril. It would protect itself.

Where does the money go?

A significant flight of deposits from the Québec banking system to American currency is plausible. Look at Figure 2 (page 140), and the monetary masses at stake. Only a slight displacement of individual savings would suffice to precipitate a liquidity crisis. The Caisse de dépôt does not have enough liquidity to neutralize it. The Québec government would be powerless. In addition, it would be a large borrower. The banks, also, conscious of the fragility of the service entente with the Bank of Canada, would limit their risks. The liquidity crisis would arrive in a few days.

Does this lead to a Québec currency?

Yes. What follows would be predictable. The Québec economy would risk paralysis from the liquidity crisis. The government would have to act rapidly. It would issue a quasi currency, Québec "dollars," assuring full convertibility into Canadian dollars. Those who are not able to find Canadian dollars will fall back on this Québec currency. Initially the government would maintain parity. But the exchange would be complicated, bound up with bureaucratic controls to prevent speculation. In the space of several days, Québec dollars would be transacted at a discount and would be devalued *de facto*. Unable to support all monetary transactions by maintaining parity, the Québec government would progressively limit conversions at parity. And as soon as the necessary mechanisms exist, it would abandon convertibility. An emergency law on Québec currency would simply sanction everything. Thus Québec would have its own currency, in a brutal manner, and in the space of some weeks. It is always in this way, in the disorder and the atmosphere of crisis, that new currencies are born in monetary economies.

And what would follow?

The disorder is hard to describe or predict. Never has such an operation been attempted in an economy as advanced as Québec's. Existing contracts and financial engagements are stated in Canadian dollars. Their value would diminish with the devaluation of the Québec dollar, as legal tender would be changed. The Québec government would probably want to protect itself against the costs of this devaluation. In that special emergency law, it could also convert its own engagements and those of the agencies it controls, like the Québec Pension Plan and the Workmen's Compensation Board, automobile insurance and health insurance authorities, into Québec dollars. This could result in lawsuits on the part of pensioners, particularly those who live outside of Québec. Many Québec businesses would be squeezed, with accounts payable to suppliers in Canadian dollars and accounts receivable from clients in Québec dollars. Devaluations always cause misery. This is stiff medicine, albeit profoundly unjust medicine.

And after that?

Following the devaluation, inflation would spring up. Devaluations also always lead to inflationary pushes, as the price of imported goods rises. Imports represent about one-third of the goods and services sold in Québec. The government would also want to inject some liquidity into the banking system, especially because this would facilitate its own financial operations. Unfortunately, one side-effect of such a policy is inflationary pressures. All new currencies begin their "careers" with an inflationary push. Savers — who would have kept their savings in Québec dollars — would pay the price as the value of their savings would shrink.

All countries who became independent in the past 50 years have ended up with their own currency. All countries, with the exception of Singapore, have financed their accession to independence on the backs of their savers, with inflation. Return to Figure 2 (page 140). Where is the money? With the government? No. In the financial institutions? No. There are nearly as many debts as assets. In the Caisse de dépôt et de placement? No. There is only one account largely in surplus: the savings of households. In most countries, governments have generally financed accession to independence with these savings. Hardly surprising that savers lack trust and place their savings far from governmental claws in a currency that the latter does not control! Slovakia, the Baltics, and the Ukraine are recent examples. Monetary union would be a temporary respite, lasting no more than a few weeks. Relentless inflation would eventually "arrange" the implicit transfer of funds from savers to governments.

But Québec is not Slovakia.

Of course. But the conditions would be even more propitious in Québec than in Slovakia for a monetary crisis. Private savings are more preponderant. Our governments are more "broke." And we have electronic transfers of funds. Banking crises are short and sharp. The 1992 negotiations between Slovakia and the Czech Republic were supposed to lead to a common currency, basically to calm savers in Slovakia. The entente was not credible, for the same reasons as the one between Canada and Québec would not be credible. The crisis was swift. The entente came into being on January 1, 1993. Two weeks later, the Slovakian banks were dry of cash. And 38 days after officially launching their currency union, the two governments called the whole thing off. The people had won. The Czech and Slovakian common currency scheme did not last six weeks!

If you still don't believe it, look at the Swedes, who went through a monetary crisis, although it did not involve a common currency. "That can not happen to us! We are a rich country. We have friends. We have savings. We are not foolish!" Oops! They end up with interest rates of 500% for a weekend. And credit crunches. Sure it cannot happen to the Swedes! Well it did.

The conditions in Sweden in many ways were similar to those in Québec. The numbers did not add up; there were significant reservoirs of individual savings; government was spending too much and it owed too much money, much of it to nervous foreigners; there was a deficit in the current account balance; and money was "electronic." The house of cards collapsed because of a little crisis in a neighbouring country, Finland. But they did not believe it.

What would a separate and devalued currency mean for Québecers?

Another mess, for Québecers and for all those who have financial contracts and agreements written in Québec. Remember that in many of our contracts we specify which laws apply, or in which judicial district they have been signed. That would create problems. Suddenly these contracts would change from Canadian dollars to Québec dollars, worth 15% less, or maybe even less than that. A mess.

And a costly situation for Québecers who would see the value of their savings devalued in terms of their purchasing power outside Québec. Look at what has recently happened in Mexico. This is not fun.

Finally, inflation would take hold. Too many prices would be fixed internationally. That is enough to kickstart an inflationary spiral if the government is not careful with the printing press. And countries faced with the deficit and the demand for liquidity usually aren't. New currencies generally start with an inflationary binge. A terrible mess for the little guy.

17

The Aboriginal Peoples

David Johnston: *Let's now turn to a complex problem you have referred to several occasions earlier: the aboriginal peoples. You wish to begin with a story, and before that with a book.*

Marcel Côté: The book was published in Great Britain: a large book that helped us discover the richness of Québec; an eloquent book. The author, a respected writer, presents Québec and Québecers in a manner that few writers have been able to do. Not only does he know Québec, he extensively interviewed experts on Québec society: historians, sociologists, and economists. He managed to translate, in clear language, the reality of Québec, today and yesterday.

Edited by one of the largest publishing houses in the country, the book is magnificent, with an exceptional choice of beautiful images, well reproduced. The paper is beautiful. The binding is rich and elegant. The cover photograph, a magnificent view of Québec, entices one to open the book.

This is a book that the premier of Québec offers to important visitors. This is a present we all want to give to visiting friends who discover Québec. One of Britain's leading corporations, with significant operations in Québec, offered it as a Christmas present to its 500 most important clients.

Nonetheless, Québecers ignore the book. In fact, no respecting Québecer could like it. Its title stings: *Cabot's Land*. The author ignores the name of our country, Québec. Cabot is the explorer who, in the name of the King of England, discovered Québec in the sixteenth century. Adopting the suggestion of a great historian, the author rebaptizes Québec as Cabot's Land, the name of one who symbolizes all who gave Québec its rule of law, democratic institutions, modern economy, transportation, hospitals, much of its culture.

But it is not the name that Québecers give their country. It could never be the name of an English explorer who did not even speak their language. How could the author think that Québec did not have a name? How could he have the reflexes of a colonizer and see only his own reality?

This is fiction.

Yes. The book *Cabot's Land* doesn't exist. How could anyone write a book on Québec that renames Québec after an English explorer? This would be truly to misunderstand Québec.

But in reality this book exists, under another title: *La Radissonnerie*. It's a magnificent book on James Bay. It's a big book with exceptional images of this northern land. The authors give voice to historians, ethnologists, aboriginal elders, storytellers, hopeful youths. If you really want to know James Bay country, read this book. But forget the title, which is a terrible mistake.

Surprisingly, the author is proud of his choice of name for this vast country. The suggestion was made initially by two Québec social scientists, Louis Edmond Hamelin and Roger Lejeune, two specialists of the middle-north. Radisson was the first white person to explore the territories around James Bay, a coureur de bois who worked for the King of England. A splendid name, says the author, who hopes it will seep into common usage. Moreover, did the government not name the administrative capital of the region, a little village near the La Grande 2 Dam, Radisson?

The Québec premier probably offered the book to his distinguished guests. Hydro-Québec must also have offered it to those visiting its hydro installations. The book is available in college and university libraries.

No one I know noticed anything terribly wrong in the name: neither the author, nor the editor, nor any who offered the book as a gift, nor newspapers who critiqued the book, nor booksellers who publicized it.

But consider what the Crees think of this new name for their land, the name of the white man who "discovered" them. What an honour! What a beautiful name for their country, that already had a name for over 5000 years, a Cree name, Ernu Astchee.

That we white Québecers find nothing abnormal in *La Radissonnerie*, to the point of silence, signifies the great divide that separates us from the aboriginal peoples who share the Québec territory with us. Perhaps now is the time for us to realize the consequences of the sharing of this country by more than one nation.

Let us transfer ourselves into the classroom of a North American Indian professor explaining to white North Americans, and especially to Québecers, the attitude of aboriginal peoples towards the independence of Québec.

THE INDIANS' COUNTRY

We are 2.3 million in North America, 500,000 in Canada. In Québec we are approximately 60,000, divided among ten nations, or tribes as you occasionally say. Add approximately 10,000 Inuit, who are not Indian and who live in the North. The nation, for an Indian, is like a people for you, the whites. You are Americans or Canadians or Québecers. We, Indians, are Cree, Dene, Huron, etc. Peoples and nations are roughly the same. They are also equal. Our Indian nations are smaller than your peoples, but this does not alter reality.

Traditionally, we were nomadic. We lived principally from hunting and fishing on ancestral territories which were relatively well defined. The arrival of the whites in North America provoked an immense shock to all the Indian nations. You pushed us around. You occupied our lands. White civilization also had a devastating effect on our civilization. The whites attacked us not only with guns, but also with alcohol. And you almost managed to destroy us. Nonetheless, white civilization brought benefits. Our generation lives much better than our ancestors. But this is also the case for the whites, is it not? On the other hand, illness, alcoholism, drug addiction, idleness, and violence continue to ravage the Indian nations of North America. Today's Indian, whether Dene, Cree, or Apache, is faced with enormous problems of adaptation. But we have decided to take hold of ourselves.

We are not and will not become white. We are proud to be Indian. Have no illusions. Even if we sometimes speak your language, we remain Indian. We constitute America's First Nations. There are, moreover, no "Québécois Indians." It is not because you came to live on our lands that we have abdicated who we are or that we will cease to be Indian and will become "Québécois." All Indians already have a nation.

For 400 years we have shared our territory with the whites. Remember guns and alcohol. We have accepted your presence, but not as colonialists. We have rights, rights which do not derive from you. These are rights of sovereign nations, of Indian nations of America. Each Indian nation has historical territories which are divided among various bands of the nation. Our bands are like your cities.

If the white has his or her country, the Indian has his or her territory. A territory is unlike your country, a geographical area on a map with cities, frontiers, and governments. Our "country" is the territory that our ancestors left us: the lakes and the forests that our father helped us discover when we were children. Even if an Indian nation comprises only 5000 Indians, it has a territory and they are as important as your country. This is another reality to which you must become accustomed.

Our country, therefore, cannot be Québec or Canada. If we live in what you call your country, it is because you have imposed your reality on ours, with the assistance of guns and alcohol. But our reality remains.

The whites often think their problems are more important than ours. Like we should worry about the Canadian

constitution. But have you ever visited one of our communities? Are you aware of the conditions in which our youth
live? This can no longer be. We must take care of our
problems. This is our priority. We have concluded that only
Indians can find the solutions to eradicate themselves from
this state. White paternalism is a failure.

For this reason, we speak of rights and sovereignty. Not
only in Québec. Aboriginal peoples across North America
are living a quiet revolution. The time has come to reclaim
our rights, to rediscover our territories, to reject the colonizer,
to engage in a new dialogue with whites.

For this reason, Oka was important for North American
Indians. We stood up to the whites. They wanted to build a
golf club on an ancestral burial ground. A golf club! As if
the whites did not already have enough! Indians came from
all across North America to support our brothers at Oka
who fought for their rights. And we won. The whites' golf
club was not built.

We are also proud of Elijah Harper, the Cree Indian who
blocked the Meech Lake Accord by rising, feather in his
hand, to say simply no, to consideration by the Manitoba
Legislative Assembly of the Meech Lake Accord. The white
people of Canada wanted to settle their differences and
regulate their problems without solving ours. Impossible.
They must recognize us. No longer will the North American
Indian accept that white people reconstruct their country
without taking into consideration our nations and our
territories. The Indians blocked Meech. They also voted
against the Charlottetown Accord, despite the support of

some Indian chiefs. They also oppose Québec independence, unless the sovereignty of their nations and their territories is recognized.

The white separatists of Québec want to transfer our territories from Canada to Québec, as if our nations were colonies. The Indians will not accept to change from a "white" country to another one without their consent. We are not baseball players, tradable according to the owners' wishes. Our territories belong to no one other than the Indian nations.

As long as the whites of Québec do not recognize our sovereignty on our territories, the Indian nations will oppose all constitutional change. We are patient. Our problems are also as important as yours.

The Québec government perhaps thinks that it is capable of buying the support of Indians, particularly those who speak French. Money has replaced alcohol. But it is not because they speak French like Québecers that the Odanak, Hurons, or Montagnais are less Indian. They are perhaps more disposed to have confidence in the Québec government, which in fact is probably more progressive than most of the other governments of Canada. But it would be a big error to believe that this understanding extends to accepting the tutelage. No Indian nation will again trade its sovereignty and its rights. Have no illusions: Indians also want their sovereignty, at the same time as you.

The Indian nations of Québec will thus be quite united faced with the question of independence. Those who have traditionally spoken English — the Mohawks, Cree, Mic Mac, and many Innu and Algonquins — historically distrust the Québec government. But all Indian nations distrust white governments, make no mistake about it. So long as their sovereignty is unrecognized and new treaties, nation to nation, unsigned, they will prefer the status quo. They will refuse to be exchanged. They will oppose the transfer of their territory from one country, Canada, to another, Québec.

The error of the whites is to believe that the recognition of the territorial jurisdiction of Québec as a country is a legal question, regulated by international law. Is there a spectacle as sublimely ridiculous as the learned testimonies of international jurists with treatises and treaties in hand, arguing before the parliamentary commissions that an independent Québec would have the right to the territorial integrity of the province of Québec. The Québec government reclaims with such testimonies a timeless recipe that was used against us many times in the past. Force always manifests itself to mask its past; solicitors replace soldiers; robes replace rifles. But neither jurists nor soldiers will regulate this problem.

The error of the whites is to underestimate the world today. The Indians to whom you feel superior will teach you a lesson. Guns and whiskey have lost their potency. This is the age of television and the quill. These are the weapons natives use to defend themselves today. Television and the quill. Remember Elijah Harper and his feather. Meech fell in a few days.

The Indian nations will oppose the transfer of their territory from the tutelage of one white government to another, without their consent. While the white jurists conduct their little spectacle of servility, our chiefs will seek television, quill of peace in hand, to affirm their own universal symbol, their historic right to self-determination and control of their ancestral territories, of which they are still the sole master. White jurists will probably laugh, seeing there only a spectacle of feathers and ancestral drums. But you will see who will win.

The Mohawk nation, well known for its belligerent tradition, is likely to be first to refuse to recognize the sovereignty of Québec on its own territory and its transfer of jurisdiction to the new republic. The Crees will follow, combatting the transfer with their lawyers, with legal procedures, and with media interventions on a world scale. Most of the Indian nations of Québec will opt for the same strategy, maintenance of the status quo, so long as their sovereignty is unrecognized. If Québec persists in its independence pilgrimage, it will be challenged over the major part of its territory, by the Indians, and farther north, by the Inuit.

Certain commentators reject with the back of their hand the sovereignty claims of the Indian nations. They say we are only 60,000 in Québec, dispersed in ten tribes. How could we claim to constitute nations? How can we form a country? Our aspirations to sovereignty, according to these observers, would only be a manoeuvre orchestrated by the rest of Canada to deny to Québecers the integrity of their territory. Québec must reject sovereignty claims, conclude these observers. How ignorant these people who call themselves experts!

Are the Indians the puppets of the enemies of Québec? Evidently not. But is this important? In truth, no. The Indians will march to their own drum, doing what they have to do, whatever the motives one imputes to them. The important thing for Québecers is to realize what we, the Indians of North America, will resist if your government insists on trying to transfer us from one white country to another one, without our consent and without recognizing our full sovereignty on the territories that we Indians consider ours.

Québecers think of themselves as "good whites." They like to remind us that they treat us better than the other provinces. But the colonizer always ignores the ignominy of his situation. The Indian will not change masters. Not at the dawn of the twenty-first century.

Indians are not violent. They do not approve of armed interventions. Perhaps the Mohawks made a lot of noise at Oka. But that is their tradition. Remember the weapons of the twenty-first century: the television and the quill. The Indians will make a call to the world's conscience and for the solidarity of all the people who have known exploitation and colonization.

We can block the recognition of Québec by international organizations. At the United Nations, a single Security Council veto suffices. We shall have several. Without U.N.

recognition, recognition of Québec elsewhere will be difficult.

The Americans, Germans, and Scandinavians will also help us in international organizations, particularly in the International Monetary Fund and the World Bank. No question of recognizing Québec before an agreement with the Indians.

Even France would hesitate. The Indians are popular in France, as Québecers are. The Indians of Québec speak French as well as Québecers.

But it is in the United States where the battle will be fought. Québec needs the United States, to finance its debt and to buy its exports. We can block the entry of Québec into NAFTA; the free trade agreement. The U.S. Senate will never agree to vote for an anti-Indian treaty. That is unthinkable. A vigil at the entrance of the U.S. capital, with feathers and drums and our political message will be heard! A comical spectacle, the white jurists will say. But you will see there a profound symbolic message which will touch the American voters. The senators will understand.

But the debt will cause the greatest surprises for the Québec government. Québec is a large borrower in the United States. You know it. We also know it. We also know who the buyers of Québec bonds are. They are principally pension funds, on the east coast of the U.S. and in California. They will heed the Indians' voice. Have no illusions.

We also have our allies in the state legislatures and in the American congress. We shall demand a boycott of Québec bonds. We shall demand a boycott of the brokers who sell Québec bonds. We shall demand a boycott of the businesses whose pension funds buy Québec bonds.

Picture our campaign: "Cowboy and Indian games are over. Do not finance the oppressors of Indians." "The Indians have suffered enough: boycott Québec." "Wounded Knee is sufficient: say no to oppression." Hollywood actors will donate their time. The most celebrated publicity agencies will seek us out to produce our commercials. This will be "the cause" to rally around. We know about the sense of guilt felt by American whites towards Indians. Finally, they can exculpate themselves. Happily for them the "wicked ones" will not be American. It will be so easy for them to be on the good side, simply by saying "no" to Québec. Good luck to those who wish to sell their bonds, or even Québec products, in the United States.

No, you will not go forward on the back of the Indian nations. If you want your sovereignty, you will have to recognize ours as well!

18

Too Many Things at Once

David Johnston: *How can you be so certain of this litany of costs and crises?*

Marcel Côté: I looked at the real economy and identified the areas and sectors that have been most disturbed by changes of country, and examined how big the disturbance was. Then I looked at monetary policy and at fiscal policy, and added up the numbers.

But one can also look at history and read it through clear eyes. A country never becomes independent without a major economic impact. The costs of reorganization and dislocation must be paid. Diverse sectors of the economy must reorganize following changes in the legal framework. This is true for Québec, as it was for Slovakia, Ukraine, the Baltics and others.

But each case is particular. Surely comparisons must be made with care.

Of course. But divorces without transition costs are rare, save when they sanction separations that already exist in fact. In the case of Québec and Canada, we are still very united, by a delicate web of economic, political, and social considerations. Many are the filaments that would be twisted or broken by separation of this historic community. The resulting costs are considerable. And both monetary and fiscal policies will just worsen them.

We are now experts on the question of costs of independence. How would the divorce happen?

Let's answer by examining Figure 3, a variation of Figure 1 presented in Chapter 6. We see here all the forces of adjustment that converge on the Québec economy, if the government follows its independence project. Let's undertake an impact analysis. Let's examine the project chronologically from the perspective of two cities, Montréal and Chicoutimi. The choice of these two cities is not arbitrary. Montréal will be the first city touched by economic restructuring of independence, because of the anglophones. Chicoutimi, where the economy depends in large part on exports and governmental activities, will be affected much later by restructuring consequences.

To set our scene, imagine that the Parti Québécois has won its referendum some time ago. English Canada has at last succeeded in agreeing on a mandate of negotiation. It is evidently a matter of a big "if," scarcely realistic, but nevertheless, it is a possibility. Moreover, certain Québec separatists think that this is possible. For the sake of discussion, let's take them at their word.

So the negotiations to break Canada into two countries begin?

Yes. The number of topics to negotiate is very large. One must parti-

Figure 3
Convergence of economic pressures

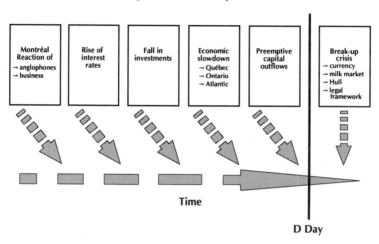

| Montréal Reaction of → anglophones → business | Rise of interest rates | Fall in investments | Economic slowdown → Québec → Ontario → Atlantic | Preemptive capital outflows | Break-up crisis → currency → milk market → Hull → legal framework |

Time

D Day

tion debt, rewrite international and inter-Canadian ententes, divide federal government activities and establish a Québec program to absorb them, negotiate civil servant transfer, hand over tax accounts, conclude a common-market accord, come to agreement with the aboriginals. One must also regulate thorny questions like the transport of electricity from Churchill Falls, an important point for Newfoundland, and the St. Lawrence Seaway, a major concern for Ontario. No one should have illusions: the negotiations will be difficult. The gauntlet has been thrown.

As soon as formal negotiations begin, Canada's breakup becomes more and more of a certitude for people. People begin to prepare mentally for Québec's separation. Costs of transfer rise from the shadows.

And we see them first in Montréal?

Yes. Beginning with increases in departures of anglophones and reorganization and relocation of businesses. Accepting that independence will be a *fait accompli* in one year or two, many citizens and businesses jump the queue and are first to the gate. Anglophones, who have no intention of remaining, promptly put their houses up for sale, before the real-estate market founders.

The breach in the Montréal economy opens immediately. It grows quickly. Anglophones begin looking elsewhere. They number 800,000. Businesses with Montréal head offices begin to reorganize their operations, quietly relocating the Canadian part of their head offices, along with treasury activities. Lawyers' and accountants' offices doing business with these head offices prepare to reduce their activities. Many anglophone professionals also follow their clients to Ontario. The real-estate market in the city centre is also affected. From the first days of negotiations, one senses the slow down in Montréal like the quiet before the storm, even though officially nothing has changed.

And people in Hull and Gatineau?

They, too, are affected early by preemptive adaptations by the anglophones in the region, with similar consequences for real-estate. In the rural area one also notes the effects, first with a rapid drop in land prices. In Chicoutimi, life continues in its normal fashion. Plants that ship their products around the world continue to operate at full speed. Elsewhere in the province the dairy farmers start to prepare for the collapse of the Canadian supply management plan. The big Québec milk cooperatives anxiously look elsewhere in Canada for milk processing plants to buy, to absorb the loss of half of their

Québec quota and for access to the English-Canadian market. They wait, however, till the last minute to close their Québec factories. The slowdown in Montréal and in the Outaouais is not yet sufficiently deep to qualify as a recession. The Montréal crisis has not yet reached full boil. Taxes continue to be paid to Ottawa and Québec. Fiscal policies of the two governments do not change. But large movements are under way. Perspicacious analysts discern the early trembles of the recession of transition. Interest rates begin to rise.

Led by the Bank of Canada?

The Bank of Canada is at the ready. Financial markets are increasingly nervous faced with the possibility that Canada could break up. To appease lenders and finance the current deficits of the federal and provincial governments — $60-billion annually — the Bank of Canada must hike interest rates. If not, a financial panic could break out.

What specifically does the Bank of Canada do?

It raises interest rates a further 0.5% above U.S. rates. This temporarily comforts holders of Canadian debt who are uncertain about the final entente, about the negotiations on the debt, and about the impact on the Canadian economy of these large changes. But the premium that comforts the lender worries the borrower. The 0.5% premium costs governments an additional $4-billion per year, or $150 per citizen. The effect of this hike diffuses slowly through the economy. A delay of six months to one year is normal as investors and borrowers in general adjust their plans to these higher rates. In the Montréal area, businesses face more important problems than these increases in interest rates. Construction is down, retail sales are down, people do not spend. The mood is gloomy. In Chicoutimi people don't believe the increase in interest rates is due to the negotiations with the rest of Canada. "After all, nothing has changed and Alcan is still hiring!" Elsewhere in Canada, the search for a guilty party has started: It's Québec's fault. Resentment spreads like a brushfire.

And what about the negotiations?

The various elements of the entente become clearer and clearer, in keeping with accelerating negotiations. Indeed, Mr. Parizeau can announce there is definite progress. At one press conference he suggests a probable date for the official transfer of power. The media shock is profound. "A deal is in the making. Independence will truly occur." The Canadian dollar drops by one cent. The Bank of Canada intervenes again, and interest rates rise. The general population, the business community, and investors prognosticate the details of the negotiation, the stakes and probable compromises. Sovereignty slowly become a certainty for everyone. The probable outcome sinks in. It serves nothing to wait. One must adjust.

This realization creates a shock in the Montréal economy. Businesses rapidly reorganize. Within a few months hundreds of Québec affiliates are created, with their own head offices. But parallel to this, the Canadian head offices are moved out. Service activities to these businesses are also profoundly affected. There are significant job losses in the downtown office towers. Retail businesses are also greatly affected. Individuals also leave the city, in spite of the great difficulty in finding buyers for their homes. Bank deposits are transferred out of Québec. For an anglophone, to remain in Montréal is to become a minority, to cease to live in English. The anglophone hospitals are in crisis. No one wants to be the last "English" in Montréal. Immigration into Québec drops. The climate is morose. Alliance-Québec demands a new referendum.

Simultaneously, many businesses with Canada-wide commercial arrangements — for example, defence industries, dairy products — adjust to the new reality emerging from the negotiations: two countries, two markets. They drop back on investments in Québec, downsize personnel, reduce inventories, and spread out production to keep their facilities open. Money flows out.

Québec businesses that depend on Canadian markets begin to feel a slowdown. Small and medium-size manufacturers are hit particularly hard. The whole Canadian economy turns at a slower rhythm, because of interest levels and uncertainty. The "backlash" against Québec products is also growing.

At Chicoutimi, people still speak enthusiastically of independence, though owners of small and medium-size enterprises beg to differ. But no real economic downturn is felt yet, save for among the graduates of the University of Québec at Chicoutimi who seem to have more difficulty finding a job this year. The fault lines slowly spread from Montréal across the Québec economy.

Do these effects not feed back into the negotiations?

Yes, for some weeks negotiations have become "virile." Accusations of bad faith multiply. Negotiations are stymied on the Canadian debt. Canada insists that its repayment has preference over the Québec debt. Québec ends up ceding this point. In return, Canada consents to an administrative entente on the native peoples, insofar as any judgements from Canadian tribunals do not supersede it. Québec agrees to an army of 25,000 men, integrated partially with Canadian forces. Canada will support Québec's request to join NAFTA if a full entente is reached on all topics. But the Bank of Canada insists that Québec contribute $3-billion to a stabilization fund to defend the Canadian dollar and ensure liquidities in Québec. Ottawa will require Canadian residency for those who would work in the Canadian public service, a hard blow for residents of the Outaouais. The project of joint currency management is also remitted *sine die*. Canada insists on keeping the full authority of the Bank for now. Finally the milk producers have their funeral. They have just sustained the hit that explodes their industry: from "D Day" they will be excluded from the Canadian supply management plan for industrial milk. The whole rural economy prepares for the aftershocks.

And in Montréal and Chicoutimi?

Unemployment has climbed by 5% in Montréal. No one agrees on the number of anglophones who have left. But the real-estate market is totally on its back and the departures continue. Defence enterprises demand guarantees from the Québec government to continue production. In the Outaouais, municipalities organize a referendum to join Ontario. The Québec government announces an austerity plan. The salaries of public servants are unilaterally reduced by 10% for a period of three years. Rumours float of a 1% tax on wealth. One sees massive transfers of registered retirement savings plans to Ontario accounts.

In Chicoutimi people begin to see the effects of the crisis taking on strength in the heartland of Québec and around Montréal. Unemployment is growing. Some industrialists confirm that they have lost contracts in Ontario. The public service unions prepare to demonstrate against the salary cuts. "No one told us anything about that!" one hears. But the smelters and the paper mills keep on churning, thanks to strong export markets.

And finally the Québec-Canada negotiations produce an agreement and "D day" arrives.
The celebrations are not very successful. In Montréal there are more protesters than people who support the government. In New York, Robert Kennedy, Jr., declares that it is a sad day. He announces that he will propose a law to prevent the purchase of Québec bonds by United States pension funds, as long as Québec doesn't arrive at an agreement with the native peoples. There is also no question of the U.S. accepting Québec into NAFTA without an satisfactory entente with the aboriginals.

Québecers are just starting to get used to Québec government coupons, which have served for money for some weeks. A wealth tax is announced. Registered retirement savings plans will be hit, as many feared. In Chicoutimi the recession has arrived, nearly one year after it hit Montréal. The government lays off 500 public servants in Chicoutimi, a big shock to the community.

Dairy products plants have shipped their last truckload to Ontario. The solidarity plan of the milk producers, which is supposed to spread the burden of the loss of the Canadian market, is not functioning well. Producers are unhappy with the level of the Québec subsidy, which covers only 25% of their loss. In Hull the community is crushed. The Canadian government has announced that the new rules of residence will apply three months from now in the national capital region.

The two last torpedoes have thus exploded. Their impact will reverberate over several years through the Québec economy.

The transfer of old-age pensions and allocations to veterans is supposed to take place in a month, according to the government of Québec. But it has also announced its intention to pay in coupons and not in Canadian dollars. Coupons are exchanged presently at 80 cents on the dollar on the street. Credit unions will cash no more than $100 per client per week. "The government will not guarantee more," the Caisses insist.

In Chicoutimi a new political movement is created to rejoin Canada!

How realistic is this scenario?

Partisans of independence will find it too bleak. But it is quite possible. Happily, though, it is not all that probable. For it ignores the political reality of Québec and of Canada, of the difficulties of the negotiations and of arriving at an entente, as much with English Canada as with the native peoples. And of the patience of Québecers, which would become tested past the breaking point, and put a stop to the nonsense.

19

The Emperor Has No Clothes

David Johnston: *Let me draw your attention to three of the 19 clauses in the question proposed by the government of Québec for the referendum quote: clause 1: Québec is a sovereign country; clause 2: The government of Québec has the mandate to negotiate an economic association with Canada immediately after a positive response at the referendum; clause 16: The present law will be enacted one year after its approval by referendum, unless the National Assembly determines an earlier date. Does this mean that under any circumstance, whether there is an agreement or not, Québec becomes an independent country within one year after the referendum, presuming the separatists win it?*

Marcel Côté: That is what the proposal says.

Is it possible?

Anything is possible. But it is highly improbable. Indeed, this would be folly. The threat of a unilateral declaration on the part of Québec, incorporated in a referendum question, is only a gambit in the search for a hard mandate for negotiations, a convincing mandate that would budge Canada. The péquiste government really does not want to declare unilateral independence for Québec. If it makes this threat, it is probably only to ease negotiations.

So the threat of a unilateral declaration would just be a bluff?
Yes, a bluff that is most likely to be quickly unmasked when the chips are down.

Would the government dare to put its threat into operation?
No, I think not. The consequences are too serious. The threat of unilateral declaration, even if it is incorporated in a referendum question, would also quickly be perceived as a bluff. On prudent examination the government could also decide not to incorporate it into a referendum question because it would only be a cause of subsequent humiliation and loss of face in the negotiations, in the case of victory of the separatist option.

But as you have described earlier, just leading Canada to the negotiating table would be a formidable challenge.
Yes, as we saw at the beginning of our conversation, there are several fundamental difficulties in bringing Canada to the negotiating table, whatever may be its mandate to negotiate. First there would be the case of Jean Chrétien, MP from Québec, to sort out. Then the necessity of a unanimous agreement among the nine provinces to decide on a mandate with which to approach Québec. Furthermore, the prov-

inces will be much more interested in an entente among themselves to reorganize a new Canada than in a separation entente with Québec. The "Canada" accord, in a world run by politicians, will take precedence over the "Québec separation pact."

Then the aboriginals would pose legal and political problems that one should not underestimate.

Finally, these ententes will likely require the unanimous accord of the nine provinces and of the federal government to enter into force. Two or three provincial elections expected over the next several years would make it difficult, if not impossible, to reach such unanimity.

And what does Mr. Parizeau do during this hiatus?

He waits, impatiently and for a long time, to begin his negotiations. If nothing is done to quicken the will to negotiate within the rest of Canada, centred on restructuring the federation with nine provinces and three territories, the negotiations with Québec may not begin. It is not a matter of bad faith on the Canadian side. Rather, the Canadians would have divergent interests and priorities, collectively the opposite of Québec. Simple pursuit of legitimate political interests may prevent negotiations from even beginning.

Most analysts from Canada share such a conclusion. This is also why many Québec separatists propose that the referendum question include an ultimatum — a date by which Québec would act unilaterally if the negotiations did not progress in a satisfactory fashion, to provide pressure and finality.

Would such an ultimatum precipitate the negotiations?

The answer is no. The commencement of negotiations requires unanimity. Threats of unilateral separation by Québec would not produce this unanimity. Too many provinces are much more preoccupied by the reorganization of Canada than by the entente with Québec. For provinces such as Newfoundland, Alberta, and B.C., unilateral separation by Québec is of lesser consequence than Canada's reorganization. Economically and politically, these provinces are not significantly affected by the unilateral withdrawal of Québec from confederation, compared with a modification of their own status in confederation. They want to regulate their situation before any settlement of Québec's situation. The aboriginals are in the same situation. It is difficult to assume that the positions of these provinces and of the aboriginals would be dramatically modified by the threat of unilateral retreat by Québec.

Then the veto of these provinces over any entente with Québec before the renegotiation of their own status would force Québec to execute its threat and proceed to its unilateral declaration of independence. Québec's bluff would be forced. What happens next?

Let's look first at the situation in the rest of Canada. We have not discussed the economic impact of the separation of Québec on Canada. We must leave detailed analysis of this for another time. But the impact would be dramatic! In a divorce, both parties suffer. Canada would also find itself in a difficult economic situation. A country with 128 years of remarkable history, perhaps the most civil, the envy of the world, would be broken asunder. Although the disturbances would be less pronounced than in Québec, both in absolute and relative terms, the effects would be deeply damaging. They would create serious political problems, particularly in the Atlantic provinces and in Ontario.

Could you briefly identify these effects?

Hikes in interest rates would be the first negative impact. The noxious effects of this would be felt most severely in every region of the country. Canada's high rate of indebtedness and the uncertainty of Québec participation in federal debt repayment would force the Bank of Canada to adopt a very prudent attitude, to conserve the confidence of lenders. The additional interest costs would create serious fiscal pressures. Canadian and provincial governments would be obliged to reduce their deficits more rapidly. In other words, constitutional tensions would rapidly affect governmental fiscal policy.

The slowdown in Québec would have a significant impact on Ontario's economy, for which Québec is an important market. Indeed, the recession in Québec would precipitate one in Ontario, which would already have been weakened by the high interest rates. The same scenario repeats in the Atlantic provinces. Relocation of head offices and anglophones from Montréal to Toronto would not come close to compensating for the impact of the Québec recession on the Ontario economy.

With its tax base shrinking by 25%, the financial problems of the federal government would be felt throughout all of Canada. The federal government would probably succeed in lowering its head office expenses to accommodate the departure of Québec, but not by 25%! Canada's borrowing capacity would also be affected by the brouhaha of separation. This would increase its borrowing costs and increase the risks of a debt crisis.

The six net beneficiaries of fiscal federalism — the four Atlantic provinces, Manitoba, and Saskatchewan — risk much from a federal financial crisis. Investors would take note of those additional risks.

Thus these provinces would have more difficulty financing their debts and even refinancing the portion of their debts coming due.

Finally, a monetary crisis in Québec, as described in the preceding chapter, would put extreme pressure on the Canadian dollar, just as the crisis in Finland had repercussions in Sweden. Such a crisis in the Canadian dollar could force the Canadian government to adopt an austerity regime. The regime wouldn't be as severe as Québec's recession, but it would still have significant deflationary effects. The result: an economic recession, an increase in unemployment, bigger than we have ever known, and a drop in the value of the Canadian dollar.

Would these economic shifts affect the capacity of Canada to organize itself to negotiate the conditions of separation with Québec?

Probably not. These latter difficulties are caused by the provinces' right to veto constitutional changes and the diversity of interests across the Canadian regions. The recession would leave the aboriginals of Québec indifferent. They are not all that integrated into the market economy, so their revenues would be little affected by the slowdown. They would be little given to compromise. The provinces of British Columbia and Alberta would also be somewhat sheltered from the effects of the recession and the accompanying financial crisis because of their strong fiscal position and export-oriented economy. These provinces would also be little moved to compromise.

Up to now you have not detailed the possibility of animosity towards Québec developing in Canada. This surely could re-

sult from a Québec ultimatum, a recession, and a drastic hike in interest rates.

All that is possible, and indeed likely. Such a resentment would contribute to a hardening of attitudes by negotiators and diminish the flexibility of successful negotiation.

In light of all this, let's come back to the unilateral declaration of independence. Can the Québec government legally declare independence unilaterally?

Yes, by a simple vote of the National Assembly.

Could this result in Québec independence?

Perhaps. It would be necessary that such a declaration be accepted as much in Québec as outside to be significant. In Québec, it would be necessary for the citizens to recognize it; that would be the easy part. But citizens would have to act in consequence; that would be more difficult. It would also be necessary for Ottawa to accept it; that would be easy. And act in consequence; that would be politically risky. Finally, recognition is necessary in the international community. Such recognition is likely to depend first on an agreement with Canada, on the one hand, and with the natives peoples on the other. All this could take some time.

Let us go back to Québecers. What would they have to do to recognize the unilateral sovereignty of Québec?

Among other things they would have to decide to send their federal taxes to Québec rather than to Ottawa. This is no small decision.

Why?

If you are a convinced federalist, opposed to independence, you will hesitate. You would be caught between two legal regimes, Canada and Québec. As thousands of Québecers and Québec businesses, even hundreds of thousands hesitate, the Québec government would face important financial shortfalls. As we have seen earlier, Québec governments spending would represent 50% of the GDP. A few weeks of hesitation by taxpayers could create big problems for working capital! In fact a "taking in charge" by the Québec government of federal responsibilities without careful and planned collaboration between the two governments probably cannot take place! There are too many ongoing government programs and too much money at stake for this to be done unilaterally. For instance, government cannot stop paying old age pensions during the switch, or skipping one or two paydays for federal civil servants working in Baie Comeau during the switch. So many practical problems would pop up. Politicians who create that mess couldn't walk on the street, at least not on the same sidewalk as my mother and yours. Messes like this are just not tolerated in our society.

This is why the unilateral declaration of independence, something never seen in a country as developed as Québec, would probably be accompanied by a law suspending its application. That is, it exists as law but has not been put into full effect. The declaration could take force on June 24, 1996, but the transfer of payment of duties and taxes would only take place later, at a future date to be determined by the government in an implementing law. In the meantime, everything continues as before, including the activities in Québec of the government of Canada.

This would be incongruous!

Yes, but the Québec government would not have a real choice. To declare independence unilaterally is not that easy. In a democracy, the activities of a government cannot just stop functioning. What do you think would happen if my mother and yours suddenly no longer received their pension cheques because the two governments are bickering. The support for independence would take quite an about turn. This is what makes unilateral independence difficult in reality. It is not easy to take charge of the activities of the federal government by the Québec government in a unilateral fashion, when 10%, 20%, 30% of the population will not cooperate, not to speak of the federal government. Unilateralism sounds seductive in speeches. But has anyone really thought it through?

Would the federal government recognize unilateralism?

Not if an injunction from the Supreme Court, obtained by whatever group, like the aboriginals or veterans attached to their pensions, or by your parents or mine, in a class-action suit, prevents it from doing so. Unilateralism could function somewhat in Québec but the law continues in Canada, the other country.

This is quite confusing and highly legalistic. Is it realistic?

Where would you pay your taxes the day after? Where do you think Power Corporation and Mr. Paul Demarais or Canadian Pacific would pay their taxes, the day after the unilateral "D Day"? That's realistic enough. What would you do?

Beyond injunctions, very complex political pressures would bear on the federal government. Québec federalists would demand that the federal government not recognize Québec's unilateral decision. These federalist Québecers would be quite numerous. In their ranks would be a good part of the Liberal party's MPs in Ottawa, the leader of the Conservative party, the leader of the official opposition in Québec, and according to what the polls would say, 50% to 60% of the Québec population. These opponents to Québec independence would be ardently supported by the aboriginals and by the people of the Outaouais who would want to keep their jobs. In Canada, numerous groups might also oppose the recognition of this unilateral declaration. Newfoundland, for example, could insist that Québec first establish a corridor for Newfoundland to sell its electricity. Mr. or Mrs. Everyone, people like you or me, would find it normal that Québec and Ottawa, before accepting this unilateral action, must agree on the rules for sharing the Canadian debt.

Simple common sense would bring the prime minister of Canada to take note of the declaration of the National Assembly. But politically and legally he would be likely to take a different tack. In all likelihood he could not accommodate the unilateral calendar of the Québec government. He could persist in governing in Québec as if the declaration were only the affirmation of a wish to become independent, without immediate consequence to federal activities in Québec. Such a decision is not without consequences. After all, a quarter of federal government expenditures are made in Québec.

A unilateral declaration of independence might thus be interpreted by all parties as a declaration in principle only. If the Québec government were to go further than the principle, independence would be bought on the backs of the people and would seriously test the loyalty of citizens caught between two legal systems and drawn into a messy dispute. Neither side wishes to be embroiled in such a mess.

But would the threat of unilateral independence not have to be taken seriously and at the least lead Canada to the negotiating table more quickly?

It might accelerate things, but not necessarily to negotiate the terms of separation. A unilateral declaration could focus Canada on its own problems and priorities. It is also not certain that Québec would ameliorate its bargaining position with such an ultimatum. Québec would have encouraged hostility in some fiercely opposed groups, hardening their positions.

The possibility that Québec might repudiate or suspend its payments on its part of the Canadian debt could be a two-edged sword. We are not alone in the world. We have invited lenders to share our future. What would they say of the possibility of a unilateral declaration of independence and repudiation of the debt?

But Canada would have an interest in sensible and rapid resolution of the debt sharing question.

Yes. It even has been suggested by the Québec minister of finance that Québec would have a marked advantage to force the negotiations, by refusing to pay its part of the federal debt, until the negotiations are concluded.

Is the debt not a powerful lever? In fact, might it even be a possible deal maker for the Québec government?

Let us examine this so-called lever a little closer. The refusal of Québec to honour its part of the federal debt would only be temporary. Neighbours have to patch up their differences, especially if they are as closely integrated as Québec is with the rest of Canada. But even if it is perceived as a temporary salvo by Québec, it would provoke a debt crisis that would extend to all the provinces, including Québec. Why would international lenders trouble themselves to buy their additional Canadian or Québec debt when they do not know how or when it would reimburse their old debt? No interest premium could attract sufficient lenders to take the place of those who would leave, to attract them to buy the new debt issued by Canada and the provinces — $60-billion per year.

There would thus be a debt crisis?

Yes. And this crisis would likely arise before Québec puts any threat into execution. Financial markets are much quicker of foot than governments. With the least threat of a suspension or a repudiation of Québec participation in the federal debt servicing, the markets would react, several months before the date chosen for the unilateral declaration of independence. The first to save themselves would be the lenders! Canada and Québec would be barred from the international financial markets.

The crisis of the Canadian debt would prevent the federal and provincial governments from significant borrowing, and this right in the middle of the tussles between Québec and Canada. What do you think the attitude of Canada would be? In this standoff with Québec, what actions will Canadian public opinion dictate to its politicians? The country would be in crisis, even more severe than that faced by Sweden in 1992. The governments of all the provinces, including Québec, would have to cut their expenditures savagely because they could borrow no more and Ottawa would be in the same situation. The "national" deficit is 8% of GDP, 18% of government expenditures. Governments must have access to the financial markets to finance their current needs. Again, remember that the crisis would erupt months before the actual separation. Both levels of government would have to face their current obligations.

Wouldn't Québec be in a good bargaining position? After all, the federal government must borrow $40-billion per year, whereas the borrowing needs of Québec are only $5-billion per year. Isn't that the position Mr. Parizeau would like the federal government to be in, eager to resolve the conflict?

Let me be clear. The population and the lenders would be the hostage in that tug-of-war. Governments would not have enough money to provide their programs to the population, interest rates would increase, and the dollar would be devalued. The population, taken hostage, would be most unhappy. Lenders would also feel like hostages, with their bonds plunging in value and the risk of default zooming. The hostages are likely to turn angry.

Against whom? Against both governments, but if the lesson of the Ukraine applies, more against the Québec government. The Ukraine also thought it was a smart move to repudiate its share of the ex-USSR debt in 1991. It couldn't borrow until it finally caved in a few months later.

Your are saying that the federal government would win the tug-of-war?

It can count on the Bank of Canada, an important ally when it comes to financing. It also has a bigger domestic market for its debt, and Canadian lenders might not panic as much as foreign lenders. Ottawa could also withhold some transfer payments to Québec, 25% of its budgetary revenue, or about $2-billion in real money, every three months, a highly persuasive gesture.

Québec has recently counted on foreign lenders for over 60% of its borrowing in recent years. That window would be shut until the crisis is resolved. Some provinces may have problems financing their deficit. Both sides would try to rely on the domestic market, but I believe that there would be more solidarity on the Canadian side in supporting the federal government than there would be in Québec to support the Québec government. After all, those who control the wealth in Québec are overwhelmingly federalist.

Threatening to suspend its contribution to the federal debt would be a very big gamble for Québec, one that it would be likely to lose. If it did lose, it would have to crawl back to Ottawa with little bargaining power left. And people would be mad, both in Québec and elsewhere in Québec, for people will suffer if such a war over debt erupts. Finally, lenders would remember for years to come. They surely would not enjoy being held hostage. That would soil Québec's reputation in the international debt markets for years to come, a stupid strategy for one of the biggest international borrowers in the world. That is why I do not think that the threat of suspending payments on the federal debt will ever be made. It is too crude a bargaining tool, and it might turn against Québec.

Does that mean that unilateral independence is not in the cards?

Definitely, for it would be done on the back of the people. It would create substantial problems of governance and would turn the population against the government. This is the best way to derail independence forever.

When people start thinking about the practical aspects of a unilateral declaration of independence and of the tolls it would exact on the common people who are more dependent on government, they will put this option aside. We are a civilized society. Furthermore, governments are not suicidal.

20

Independence: Is It Possible?

David Johnston: *All right, the ultimate question: Is Québec independence possible?*

Marcel Côté: Yes, but not at any cost and not under any conditions. The Québec people would not support the costs and the disorder described in the preceding chapters, as more of the costs emerge. We do not live in an era of great patriotic sacrifices.

How can you be so sure?

Look around you. Eighteen months after an election to install a socialist regime in 1981, President Mitterrand had to execute an about face. The mounting opposition of the French people forced his hand only a few months after he launched his program. A simple consumption tax, whether it be in Japan, Australia, or Canada, can cause the government in place to lose half its electoral support. The Thatcher revolution in the U.K. was dramatically arrested when she attempted to reform the municipal tax system. She was forced to resign.

How do you account for the degree of popular support for the Québec government at the moment?

The "reality" experiment has not been tried. Thus separation is still greatly misunderstood. Moreover, as we get closer to "reality," it is unlikely that a separatist government will succeed in convincing the Québec people to follow it very far on the perilous voyage towards separation as we have explored it. So much of the electoral strategy of the separatists is to deny the gravity of the costs — for them to acknowledge their reality would be political suicide. When the costs and disorder associated with the breakup of Canada emerge into daylight, the Québec people will turn against those who have fooled them.

Can you explain how "this grand adventure," partly taken, will come to a halt?

A progressive loss of political support following mounting costs and disorder will progressively paralyse the government's action on the issue. A government can only take radical initiatives if it has popular support. Political legitimacy is essential for radical reforms. A government that has only 20% to 30% support is condemned to confine itself to current business — housekeeping. Public opinion polls at any moment in time let the people's wishes be known to the political system.

Are you saying that governments ought to govern by polls?

No, but governments must know where public opinion is situated. They cannot govern in abstraction. Their political adversaries have the same information at hand. A government today cannot follow a political agenda which a growing majority rejects. The opposition, the media, pressure groups, and the whole population will force the government to stop. There is nothing surprising in this, nor bad. It is the essence of our democratic system. We do not elect absolute kings, but rather political leaders. Their actions are subjected to numerous counterweights and constraints. And rightly so!

I do not believe the Québec government today could bring independence into being. This proposition is perhaps shocking. But the logic that supports it is unassailable. Somewhere along the long course, the Québec government will be forced to retreat in the face of eroding political support and growing costs. Just as this retreat will be inevitable, so it will be damaging for Québec interests. Québecers would be humiliated, and lose credibility. The legacy of the adventure will be animosity and bitterness, in Québec and in Canada, for everyone.

But let's examine the "grand adventure" from another angle. What then are the necessary conditions for independence?

It could be created only with the support of a "super majority" — such as 65% to 70% — and if certain conditions were fulfilled. There is a simple rule: The inevitable costs of transition connected with separation must be politically acceptable. A first step is the recognition that there will be costs, which many separatists persist in denying. On the other hand, certain of these transition costs can be attenuated by proper preventive strategies are employed. Moreover, the costs would be much more acceptable if Québec's economy were flourishing.

We have already explored the first, the actual costs. Could you examine how certain costs could be decreased?

Let us first look at the real shocks, the torpedoes described earlier. Three shocks will have brutal and quite localized effects, in Hull-Gatineau, in Montréal, and in the milk industry.

Could one constrain or neutralize the force of these shocks?

There is not much one can do to diminish Hull-Gatineau's vulnerability to Québecers' withdrawal from Canada. The principal *raison d'être* of this region is the national capital. This is its economic base. The idea of a "junior capital" is only a dream. One can conceive of reallocation of a capital as happened in Brazil, Nigeria, and soon in Germany. But has one ever observed the successful creation of a junior capital, in spite of innumerable attempts at decentralization?

How about rural Québec and dairy products?

The Québec milk industry is quite different. It could prepare for dissolution of the Canadian supply management plan and the sudden loss of the Canadian market. But time is required. Two strategies could be used.

The first would call for a planned and ordered reduction of production, to adapt the production to the smaller size of the Québec market while minimizing the loss to farmers. Québec could allow its milk producers to sell their quotas to producers in other provinces, which is illegal today. The drawback is this: it would force a significant part of the dairy products industry to relocate immediately, outside Québec, to follow its supplies of milk.

The second strategy would require rigorous cost reductions at the farm, preparing the industry for the day when it must meet international competition at half the present prices.

Neither one of these avenues would be popular with farmers. However, if the Québec government is serious about independence and wants to lessen the shock of separation to facilitate its passage, it must be ready to take such measures. Their unpopularity would be nothing in comparison with that of other measures that would plague the transition to independence.

How could one attenuate the third torpedo and the economic shock to Montréal precipitated by the departure of an important portion of the Montréal anglophone community?

Unfortunately the economic impact of such an exodus is now simply ignored. The first step again would simply be to recognize the probability of such an exodus and its potential size and impact. The preventive strategy would aim to hold the anglophone community in Montréal notwithstanding separation. The challenge would be formidable, perhaps unrealizable. But as the French sociologist Dominique Schnapper emphasized in a recent interview, an independent Québec can come into being if "the Québec political project extends beyond the ethnic-cultural definition of French-Canadians only." At present it does not integrate Anglo-Québecers. This, however, would require a major revision of their project, making a much larger place for the view and aspiration of the anglophone community. Current overtures are only small voices, with no resonance among the anglophones.

A real opening towards anglophones would require compromises that the sovereignists have not yet envisaged. Without such an overture, separation would impose costs so high to the region of Montréal that the independence project would risk suffocation and even death.

But surely separation would be much more feasible if the government could lessen the public financial crisis that would result from the repatriation of Québec expenditures and revenues from the federal government.

Yes of course. The impasse that would result from additional interest costs, from the impact of a recession the costs of which the Québec government would have to bear alone, and from the loss of advantages in Canadian fiscal federalism — all this would be much easier to absorb if the Québec government had its own finances in order. In particular it would be necessary for the provincial government to store up a significant budget surplus over some years to help it absorb these additional costs. But the Québec government currently has no manoeuvring room with regard to its own finances. It has been eating and having its cake for far too long.

A long-term strategy of modest intelligence would consist in establishing a margin of manoeuvre to absorb the shock of the additional deficit that Québec would inherit.

The prescription seems strikingly simple.

Of course. You know hard blows are coming: you make preparations, the better to absorb them. We all recognize the wisdom of the universal lesson told by Jean de La Fontaine in the fairy tale of "The Cricket and the Ant." Winter comes: it is better to make provisions. The fiscal shock of the recession would be like a long season of cruel winter storms.

Can you boil into a few points the additional budgetary costs that the government of Québec would have to bear, beyond its

current deficit and the inherited part of 25% of the federal deficit?

Here they are:

(1) A loss on the order of $3-billion in net transfers from the federal fiscal system, because we pay only 19% of taxes and duties but receive 26% of expenditures.

(2) Additional financing costs of $3-billion on the debt resulting from higher average interest costs and financing debts and in ongoing liabilities.

(3) The impact of the recession, the force of which would be borne, for the first time, uniquely by the Québec government. A 3% GDP decrease produces a supplementary deficit of $4-billion.

A government that tackles these additional overwhelming expenditures without doing its homework on its current expenses is simply not serious. How could the Québec government make cuts and tax hikes of $18-billion, if it lacks courage today, in the midst of an economic upturn, to eliminate its current $5-billion overspending? A government that contemplates separation given the current state of Québec public finances is a cricket government: it sings well but it certainly cannot survive the winter.

So the independence of Québec would be more economically imaginable if the economy were in a better state. But one might argue that economic dislocations are temporary and thus endurable.

The only separation that occurred without a major economic crisis in the twentieth century was that of Singapore. It was thrown out of Malaysia in 1965. The economy of Singapore was flourishing. It had a substantial surplus in its current account, which made it independent of foreign lenders. Québec is not in this situation. Our economy is in disequilibrium, principally due to government. The deficit on the current account of an independent Québec would initially be 8% of GDP. This is inconceivable for an independent country. This places us from the very beginning on our knees, at the mercy of international lenders. Québec would begin its life as an independent country in insolvency.

It serves no one to argue whether this is principally the fault of the federal government or the provincial government. The fact is that the Québec economy is in disequilibrium. Major adjustments would be necessary before contemplating separation. If not, the adjustments will take place by force, in conditions that we will not control and is likely to derail separation.

In fact, in our democracy it is utopian to think that politics can ignore economics. The independence project will not go forward in the current conditions of the Québec economy, no more than our overweight friends Paul and Virginia stand a chance to run the whole marathon. If the government does not have sufficient political capital or political determination to eliminate its current deficit, how do you think it could meet the immense economic and political challenges presented by this long march to independence?

21

"You, Shut Up"

David Johnston: *A great concern in this debate over Québec independence has been silence — an inability or unwillingness to discuss frankly the tough issues we have discussed in the past twenty chapters. This, to me, is enormously disconcerting. Can you explain it?*

Marcel Côté: Let me do so with a story — a true story.

Antoine Rivard was a Québec City lawyer, probably the most famous of his time. His career reached its zenith between 1930 and 1944. He was "the advocate" of the Québec region. People turned to him with the most desperate cases.

In 1944 Maurice Duplessis invited Rivard to be the Union Nationale candidate in Montmorency country, a "sure" seat. The Union Nationale was carried to power. Rivard was elected. Duplessis made him his minister of justice, a post he occupied until 1960. So far so good.

Today, one does not remember Antoine Rivard as the great lawyer of his time, nor as the minister of justice. However, he symbolizes his epoch. But for quite another reason. During a cabinet meeting, Maurice Duplessis stopped the brilliant advocate midstream with the words "You, shut up." Not wanting to cross his boss, Rivard kept quiet. Soon this got to be known. Over the years, the anecdote came to symbolize an era of great darkness, the Duplessis era.

Rivard now represents those who became silent while Québec sank into mediocrity under the Duplessis regime. While Duplessis and the traditional elite boasted that Québec had the best system of education in the world, Québec recorded an incredible backwardness. The Duplessis government conducted a witch-hunt against "communism." It denounced foreigners. At Thetford Mines, Duplessis teamed up with the petty bosses of the local asbestos mines to crush a workers' strike that became a symbol of the labour movement. When the archbishop of Montréal dared to take the part of the workers, he was sent into exile in British Columbia. "You, shut up," the system said.

The period of the great darkness certainly had its heroes, from René Lévesque to Pierre Trudeau, Michel Chartrand, Gérard Filion, and Gérard Pelletier. But they were not numerous. The great majority of the "Québec elite" during that time chose to remain silent or sing the praises of Duplessis, toeing the line before the political power which directly or indirectly told them: "You, shut up." Keep to your own affairs and say nothing. The Quiet Revolution of 1960 was required to end the great Duplessis darkness.

It is easy, forty years later, to celebrate the heroes of this period who were not frightened and who dared to confront the political correctness of the time conditioned by political power. Those who dared to contradict "le Chef" were branded "traitors, sellouts." Why? Because they did not share the opinion of the government of the time. Contrary to Antoine Rivard, they refused to be silent when the political power said to them: "You, shut up."

Unfortunately "you, shut up" is back in fashion. It's modern form is to shoot the messenger. That has even more ancient roots.

Greece in 400 B.C. was the centre of civilization, giving us, among others, Pericles, Plato, Socrates, and Alexander the Great. In that epoch Greece invented democracy, but also produced some of its crosses. In the year 481 B.C. the Greeks challenged the Persians at the Gates of Thermopylae. The Greeks were vanquished. A messenger ran to Athens to announce the bad news. "No, this cannot be. Death to the messenger," declared the political chief of Athens at the time, the tribune Alcibiades. He feared that the shock of the news would lead the Athenians to demand his resignation. The Athenians did not hear the bad news on that day. They were able to continue with their affairs, as if nothing happened. Alcibiades obtained some months' respite to preside over the politcal destiny of Athens. But killing the messenger did not change anything regarding the outcome of the battle of Thermopylae. In fact, the Athenians eventually were apprised of the bad news when reality imposed itself.

But the message passed into history. "Kill the messenger" was the weapon of Greek tyrants who did not like the ideas of their adversaries. However, in our days, one no longer murders the messengers, but assassinates their character. Don't defend the ideas which displease "the boss," because the boss will attack you personally, your motives, rather than your ideas. Messengers are assassinated today in a figurative fashion. They are branded as extremists, as sellouts, or as Duplessis did, as troublemakers. This is easier than attacking their ideas.

Plus ça change, plus c'est la même chose. The more things change, the more they remain the same. There will always be politicians who don't want people to hear the "bad news." Although killing the messenger today takes several forms, the objective is still the same: to prevent the circulation of opinions that the powers don't like. Each period has its politics of silence. Québec is now reverting to "You, shut up," that is, "Toi, tais-toi" or TTT, we would say in French.

TTT looms large in the independence debate. A New York broker suggests that the separation of Québec would create financial problems. "TTT," advise the indépendantiste leaders. "Otherwise, we will take away Québec business." And the broker is silenced.

One of the largest Canadian banks published a study which showed that if Québec separated, there would be severe economic problems. "TTT," retorted the government. "Otherwise, Québécois will cease to do business with you." This was sufficient: the bank's study was shunted aside. How strange. The independence of Québec is like the arrival of the swallows in the spring. The banks should have nothing to say on this question! Consequently all the banks and the credit unions of Québec have become neutral, silenced even if they have the custody of more than $75-billion of deposits of Québecers. Independence has nothing to do with the economy, isn't that so?

"If you speak of independence, my dear Paul, your company will lose its contracts with Hydro-Québec. You know, there are fanatics within our government who insist that you keep to your own affairs. Politics, that's not your business, isn't that so, my dear Paul?" TTT. Many business leaders who know the negative implications of independence on their own business nevertheless have understood the message. They keep quiet, and hang back in the dark.

The message spreads. TTT. The Chamber of Commerce becomes

neutral. Business people who have influence withdraw from the debate. Why involve yourself in a debate of insults and threats, a debate
that bears on individuals and reputations rather than ideas and rationale?
For twenty-five years the majority of economists who have studied
the question of the costs of independence have come to the same
conclusion: there will be important transition costs. The separatists
retort in attacking the individuals and their motivation. "Economic
terrorism. Stop stirring up fears and disturbing Québecers." TTT. Tired
from being accused of terrorism, many economists have put aside the
analysis of the costs of independence.

Little by little the field is evacuated. There remain only the separatists with their truth. "Don't worry," they say. "With the money that
we are going to save on duplications, we all pay all the costs entailed
by separation. Don't worry!"

**Can you spell out then what the indépendantistes don't want to
talk about?**

Here are fifteen questions of public interest that merit careful re-
sponses in the independence debate and that cause fear to the tenants of separation. Fifteen questions that one ought to be able to
pose without being told TTT, without being accused of terrorism.
Fifteen questions for which the indépendantistes don't like the answers.

**(1) What is the proportion of anglophones of Montreal who
could leave after separation and what would be the real cost of
this exodus be?** According to the opinion polls and according to the
leaders of the anglophone community, the proportion stands between
one-third and one-half. That is also what the examples of separation
of countries teach us. Do the indépendantistes have studies that

conclude differently? Why would anglophones not have the same attachment to their language and nationality as Québecers? Can one dismiss the economic consequences of this adjustment?

(2) How many federal civil servants residing in Québec will find a job with the government of Québec, particularly after the elimination of duplications? Can one really take seriously the promise of the Québec government to create a "junior" capital of Québec in the Outaouais? Is there a country that has succeeded in such an effort? Is it realistic to believe that the Québec government could relocate several thousands of civil service posts from Québec to the Outaouais? Will unions permit these transfers of positions? Where will the employees of the Québec region who lose their posts be relocated? Could these reorganizations be done in one or two years? And what about the studies that have tried to identify the agencies and ministries which will be transferred from Québec to Hull? Are they rigorous? Are there any? On the basis of governmental experience and studies performed for a local committee that reported to the Québec government in 1991, we have concluded that perhaps 5,000 jobs would be conserved in the Hull-Gatineau region in place of the 20,000 there now.

(3) Could Québec milk producers continue to sell their products in Canada, at double the world price, thanks to a subsidy of several hundred million dollars from Canadian consumers? It would be necessary for the Canadian parliament to amend the present law to permit Québec to continue to sell its industrial milk in Canada after independence. No politician in Canada has any interest in doing that, especially because such law would run counter to GATT and NAFTA. Can the Québec government demonstrate why Canada would continue to support industrial milk producers? Is there a more serious argument that the threat of boycotting western beef?

(4) Would the Québec industry for defence equipment survive the diminution of the defence budget in an independent Québec, as the separatists promise to do? These Québec industries would lose the Canadian government as their prime customer and likely would have to effect massive layoffs. The cuts in military expenditures that the péquiste government projects are a significant source of savings for a government forced to reduce its deficit. What is more, the Canadian government would favour Canadian suppliers for the Canadian forces. Several thousands of jobs would be affected, principally in the region of Montréal.

(5) Won't Canadian corporations headquartered in Montréal establish their "Canadian" head office outside Québec, transferring to it most of their head office activities not directly connected to Québec? Is legal continuity not required for the territory overseen by a head office? Do the American enterprises not do the same thing in establishing Canadian head offices? Has the government calculated the number of jobs which would be affected?

(6) What is the real surplus that Québecers would lose by withdrawing from Canadian fiscal federalism? Our analysis in Chapter 11 concludes that there would be a loss of $3-billion; we use official figures from Statistics Canada and government budgets. The method of allocation we used is transparent. For the transfer payments and revenues, the address on each cheque is the basis of attribution. The expenditures of service and administration are attributed according to the population base. According to this method of distribution, Québec would lose about $3-billion in repatriating these taxes and its part of the operational expenses of the federal government.

(7) What are the real savings that the Québec government

could hope to obtain from the elimination of duplications? By what methods are they calculated? According to our estimates, the Québec government could economize no more than $500- to $600-million and not the billions that it publicizes. Several methods can be used to evaluate the savings from the elimination of duplications. Whatever the method, the results converge. The transfer payments — cheques to individuals or businesses — must be excluded, for there are no duplications in these situations. The same applies to military expenses. The calculation of possible savings must take account of the value of these activities on a national basis, namely $18-billion per year. The Québec part of these expenses is based on the proportion of its population, about $4.5-billion. If 10% of what the federal government does (excluding defence) is "duplicated" by the Québec government, and the latter could replace the federal government without increasing resources or losing economies of scale, there would be a saving of $450-million. The federal government employs one civil servant per $80,000 of administrative expenditures. Savings of $500-million results in an effective cutting of about 6000 federal civil servants. Is this the number of layoffs the Québec government has in mind?

(8) What percentage of the debt and the federal deficit would Québec inherit? Based on 1994 figures, we estimate $135-billion. The principal difference between our estimate and that of Bélanger-Campeau is what percentage of the federal debt is attributed to Québec. We used Québec's share of the population rather than Québec's share of federal taxes. Can one truly claim that Québec's share of the taxes is a more acceptable basis for the two parties than share of population? It is obvious that whatever criterion is chosen, the shared percentage ought to be acceptable to the population of Canada as much as to the population of Québec. What would a neutral judge decide?

(9) What is the maximum deficit that is financeable? We estimate that the financial markets will not initially finance a deficit superior to $12- to $13-billion. This is, nevertheless, a substantial hike from present levels. Convincing demonstration to the contrary should be made.

(10) Will the cuts resulting from the restrictive fiscal policy that Québec must pursue produce a dramatic fall in internal demand and precipitate deep recession? The analysis of fiscal cuts in an independent Québec — which we estimate at $10-billion — should take account of a negative Keynesian multiplier. This not only would diminish the efficacy of the cuts but also would have a major effect on the economy. Who are the Québecers who would be touched by these cuts? Which programs would be cut? What would happen to the people touched by the recession? How does Québec intend to meet the Québec deficit in the current regime of the Unemployment Insurance Commission? Does it intend to raise the premiums, lower the benefits, or put new money into the regime? In the last case, where would it find the money?

(11) What would the impact be of a refusal by the aboriginal peoples to recognize Québec sovereignty on their traditional territories and of the international campaign they would mount to force Québec to abandon its claims? Only a few countries would dare to recognize Québec without an accord with the native peoples. Moreover, aboriginals are maintaining that they have the same right to self-determination as the Québécois.

(12) What is the likelihood that Québec would be able to use

the Canadian dollar as its currency, given the lack of confidence in the arrangement by a significant number of Québecers, the large current accounts deficit of Québec, and the lack of relevant examples in which a shared currency has worked? It would take only a small percentage of investors who had lost confidence in the arrangements and took their capital out of Québec to precipitate a liquidity crisis. Can the Québec government demonstrate that at the outset of independence, the Québec current account will not be deep in the red, due to the debt-servicing charge on the Canadian debt? What are the contingency plans, if there is a liquidity crunch in the weeks after separation, as there was in Slovakia within days of that republic's separation from the Czech Republic?

(13) Would the rest of Canada be more capable of establishing unanimity in negotiations with Québec when it has not been able to do so for the more modest reforms of the political structures of Canada? The tenants of independence ought to demonstrate that they could negotiate with the rest of Canada the conditions for the withdrawal of Québec, and that the rest of Canada would be able to agree on a common position vis-à-vis Québec within the time frame of less than four years.

(14) Could Québec obtain the consent of the United States and Canada to join NAFTA, in particular if Québec does not come to agreement in advance with the aboriginal nations? How long would that take? Québec must have the support of 67 of 100 senators, the majority required for the U.S. to admit a new member to join NAFTA. Moreover, Canada will not support the admission of Québec into NAFTA in the context of a unilateral declaration of independence, or failure to agree on the share of federal debt.

(15) Finally, would there not be border posts, with customs and immigration officers, between Canada and Québec, and restrictions on work by Québecers in Canada, a situation analogous to the current situation of Canada vis-à-vis the United States, even if there is a free trade accord? The indépendantistes suggest not much would change. Québecers would have dual citizenship. We would keep our Canadian passport. There would be no border posts between Québec and Canada. Québecers could go to work in Canada, etc. On what basis does Québec assume that there would be less restriction between Québec and Canada than exists now between Canada and the U.S?

What newly separated country has succeeded with such a *tour de force* to have its cake and eat it too?

Evading these important questions will not change the reality of the costs of transition that becoming independent will impose on Québec. The fastest way to avoid these questions is to "shoot" those who ask them, to denounce them, to marginalize them.

The avoidance of a frank discussion can lead a society into a dream world, far from the harsh realities of day-to-day life. Nothing illustrates this better than the posturing about a unilateral declaration of independence. There has not been a single study of the economic consequences, or should I say of the practical, day-to-day consequences, of such a grand gesture on the life of the governed. Has anybody ever given any thought just how seven million Québecers would be affected by this gesture? What happens to their tax refunds? What happens to their jobs? What happens to their passports, which they must renew next week? What happens to their RRSPs? To the currency? Would the government be able to borrow? Here we have a bill proposing separation tabled in the Québec legislature and sent to every Québec household, and some of the basic implications of that bill have never been studied. This testifies to the surreal and rarefied air that has been created over time by political correctness and Toi, tais-toi. This is how grand mistakes are made.

22

How Long Must We Wait?

David Johnston: *Constitutional fatigue cuts two ways — in the rest of Canada a feeling of indifference and in Québec a feeling of rejection. How do you see this fatigue?*

Marcel Côté: Québecers have been demanding constitutional changes for over 30 years, to no avail. They are getting impatient, and this is what explains the large support for the separatist option. This impatience may appear as petulance to English Canadians, who are getting tired of Québec's incessant demands, and of its preeminent role in federal politics over the past 25 years. Yet that does not change the fact that the constitutional changes which Québec has been demanding all that time, which can be summarized as a more decentralized constitutional framework, have not been met.

In 1980, during the first referendum, Québecers believed that they received promises to be heard. Two years later the Canadian constitution was repatriated and amended without their consent. Québecers, with reason, say that this would never have happened if Ontario had objected.

In 1990, the Meech Lake Accord, which repaired the wrongs of 1982, failed, under the pressure of Canadian public opinion unfavourable to Québec. Two years later, the federal government and the provinces developed the Charlottetown Accord, which aimed to please too many constituencies, and which was solidly defeated in a national referendum. Since then, most provincial governments and the federal government no longer dare to speak of the constitution. How long must Québec wait?

The Canadian federal system does not function well. One symptom is the debt crisis. The incapacity of the system to incorporate the fundamental preoccupations of a quarter of the Canadian population, and more specifically of its Québec composition, is also testimony of a profound flaw.

Some people argue that the constitutional debate is created mainly by Québec politicians, who will never be satisfied. People, even in Québec, are fed up with constitutional bickering, according to this thesis, and the rest of Canada could never satisfy Québec politicians. Unfortunately the Québec political class is a reality. Called to choose between the aspirations of this group and our federal politicians, the people of Québec would range themselves behind their own politicians.

It is most likely that as long as Canada does not reform its structures to accommodate the preoccupations of Québec, the impasse will continue. Constitutional tensions will persist and important parts of the Québec political milieu will support the idea of Québec separation. The consequences for Québec and for Canada of this impasse are serious, and far from positive for either of them.

Important resources are dissipated in this battle for power. The two levels of government do not collaborate as much as they could. The affronts are not limited to governments. The Québec electorate testifies to its dissatisfaction. In fact, the constitutional positions of the federal parties have become a major stake in the federal elections in Québec. The Liberal party of Canada was literally swept out of francophone ridings of Québec because of its constitutional positions. The official opposition is now formed by the Bloc Québécois, whose main preoccupation is the withdrawal of Québec from Canada and not the best interests of the country as a whole. The federal parliamentary system has become a prisoner of our constitutional impasse and functions poorly.

This malfunctioning creates a profound disequilibrium in the system of federal governance. Over the years, within the governing party in Ottawa, whether it was the Liberal or Progressive Conservative party, regional interests have come to dominate. Federal politics has become regional politics. Québec parliamentarians are no more guilty than other parliamentarians in that regard, but they have spearheaded this evolution. This strong regional perspective in our central government is the principal reason for the deficit problem of the federal government.

Canadians are tired of these political wars. Québecers' unhappiness with the system brought a majority of bloquistes to Ottawa. The west did the same with Reform. All over Canada, people are fed up with the constitutional agenda imposed by Québec, to a point where anglophone politicians no longer even dare to speak of constitutional reform.

But the problem will not disappear simply because one wishes. In fact, so long as there is not a major reform of the Canadian federal system, the constitutional problem will remain fundamental. It constitutes a major political stake, on the same order as jobs, whether that pleases the politicians or not. In particular there are Québecers, in Québec and in Ottawa, who will persist in keeping that issue on the front burners, pleasing no one, until Canada either reforms or breaks up. Most Québecers are also tired. This explains an important proportion of the support for separation. A true reform is the preferred option of a significant majority of Québecers. But this reform is late to come. Many Québecers have lost hope and vote for separation. Will the reform of Canada ever come, or will it only come too late?

But is it not possible that the expectations are too great, that large constitutional reform is not possible and has been successively rejected beginning with Québec's rejection of the Victoria Accord in 1971? Is it not possible that all of us must accept the Canadian federal structure as better than the alternative, and look to more modest incremental reform?
Waiting always causes anxiety. Yet, Québec federalists are condemned to wait for more favourable conditions before leading a reform of Canadian federal structures. We can always wait, but it is damaging.

But do we have the luxury of waiting? Does federalism now function so badly that you can no longer tolerate Canada?
The response is evidently no. Take culture, the most critical sector for the development of the Québec collectivity. This sector is most vulnerable to vexatious interventions of a government insensitive to Québec's priorities. The federal government is an important player in the cultural domain: CBC, Canada Council, Telefilm, the National Film Board, federal museums, and support for culture from Heritage Canada.

These interventions cost $1.5-billion, two-thirds of it for CBC. Québec obtains about one-third of these expenditures, about $500-million. This compares with Québec's budget of $500-million for such expenditures. Do Québec artists cry cultural invasion? Do Québec artists fear the federal government? The answer is no. Although a majority of the artists are separatist and would welcome the independence of Québec, the great majority recognize that the federal intervention in arts and culture actually poses no problem. In fact, people involved in culture understandably like the current two-tier system. It is not because of these "overlaps" that the artists are separatists.

In the very sensitive domain of culture, the federal intervention in Québec is accepted, recognized as sensitive and intelligent, and certainly does not constitute a menace for the flourishing of the Québec culture. The principal complaint of the cultural milieu bears on the possible diminution of the federal budget devoted to culture.

Immigration, another vulnerable sector, bears witness to what could be done within Canadian federalism.
Yes, on immigration there is very good cooperation between Ottawa and Québec. For fifteen years now, Québec has taken responsibility for attracting and choosing immigrants coming to Québec, despite the fact that immigration constitutionally devolves from the federal government. An entente signed by the Lévesque and Trudeau governments clarified the responsibilities in 1978. This is the proof that federalism can function, even when one finds two historic antagonists in power!

Is this not a good example of more modest incremental reform?
Exactly. In the social area, there is room for such reform. It is a sector

in which the two levels of government are active, but in which they both would like to cut their expenditures. As they do accusations are likely to fly back and forth between the two levels of government. But we must not lose our nerve with the protests of our politicians. They want to deflect attention from the root of their problem, their obligation to cut and be responsible to the electorate. One can expect threats, blame, and efforts to draw converts to one side. What will count is the state of the battlefield after the cuts. It is highly likely that the division of responsibilities will not change much, although politicians of one level will always blame those of the other for the cuts.

Can we afford the luxury of waiting in the economic area? Would it not be better for the management of the economy to work from a single level of government? The separatist politicians claim that Québec is wronged by Ottawa in numerous portfolios: professional training, the M.I.L. Davie shipyard, research and development budgets. Would independence allow Québec to correct these inequities?

Probably not. It is simply a question of money. Statistics show that even before interest payments, Québec receives a surplus of \$3-billion in program expenditures in relation to what it pays to Ottawa. Independentistes reply that this surplus is principally caused by transfer expenses such as unemployment insurance and transfer to the province for social programs, and not by expenditures creating jobs. Would they then recommend that the federal government cut into transfers to Québec or into unemployment insurance directed to Québecers, to invest in research and development and other expenses of this type? Where does one cut to find money? In what way would the separation of Québec be favoured if it forfeited the surplus of $3-billion that we receive from the Canadian fiscal system?

Think carefully about it! Can one really expect that an independent Québec would be better off economically, with the recession described earlier, with the problems of indebtedness concentrated on a single level of government, with a Montréal economy enfeebled by emigration, with a cannon ball shot into Hull-Gatineau and another into the dairy farms, and a monetary crisis over the market? Québecers must stop claiming that the grass is always greener on the other side of the fence!

Independence would perhaps soften the situation of the Québec politicians, who could then have complete freedom to act within Québec. It could not lessen, in the short term, our economic woes. But in fact, Québec would fall behind for several years. In the long term, we would probably return to an economic association with Canada. The modern age is given to large groupings. The Finns and the Swedes have just decided to join the European Union, not to augment their level of independence but because they recognize that they must limit their autonomy.

In the shadow of the United States, Québec will always want to associate with the rest of Canada. It sounds attractive for Québecers to argue that they are natural allies of the Americans, that Québec is the region of Canada most favourable to free trade. But Québec's interests are much closer to the rest of Canada than to those of the American giant. Even René Lévesque understood that, which is why he recommended sovereignty association. Whatever the political status of Québec might be, the majority of Québecers believe in an economic union with the rest of Canada.

Indeed, whether on the cultural, social, or economic planes, Québec's situation is not about to deteriorate under the current federal regime, in spite of all its faults. This is what should allow Québecers to be patient and to await more favourable conditions to renegotiate the terms of the Canadian federal regime.

We have spoken almost exclusively of Québec and little of Canada, particularly the understanding of Canada in Québec. Yes. Indépendantiste politicians emphasize that we can no longer wait for Canada to reform itself. Why this haste? In the cultural area, does waiting cause Québec to regress in the Canadian federal whole? In the economic area, the answer is also no. Moreover, this is why the indépendantistes themselves want economic association and a common currency with the rest of Canada.

The federal government presently faces its double problem of its deficit and its indebtedness. But one must not be hypocritical. The Québec government also has the double dilemma of debt and deficit. In fact, its problem is as large as the federal government's. If the Québec government is so efficient, why does it not prove it by eliminating its own deficit? Before proclaiming its superiority over Ottawa, the provincial level ought to demonstrate its greater discipline. This is precisely what makes the restructuring of Canadian confederation so difficult.

A deep-seated perception across Québec holds that "Canada is a two-nation country, the fruit of an historic alliance between French Canadians and English Canadians." This perception is normal when the history of Canada is analysed from a Québec perspective, strongly dominated by the linguistic distinction. But it has become, nonetheless, somewhat peculiar to Québec. In the rest of Canada, the reality of Canada has always been more complex than this duality. Even in 1867 the Atlantic provinces saw Canada as an association of provinces, three from the Atlantic and two from central Canada. The descendants of immigrants of the past one hundred years generally see Canada as a diversified country, having ten provinces and two languages, the French language being particularly confined to Québec and in federal institutions.

Although Canadians recognize that francophone Québecers form a distinct sociological entity, they do not necessarily recognize that their country is a pact between French Canadians and English Canadians, and even less between Québecers and the other provinces. They perceive their country as defined other than in relationship with Québecers. Moreover, in their eyes, English Canada is not homogeneous and they refuse to see it thus. Nova Scotia and British Columbia have as many differences between them as they do with Québec, the linguistic dimension being for them one element among many. In that regard, English Canada is truly different from Québec. The linguistic dimension is fundamental in Québec because it cements our reality as a people. Indeed, even the adjective "English" before Canada, to describe the rest of Canada, is misleading because so many language groups other than English have chosen to make Canada their home and preserve their identity.

Québecers have to restructure their vision of English Canada and recognize its complexity. It is undeniable that as far as Québecers are concerned, there will always be a "we" and "the others." But "the others" ought not to be seen as homogeneous and wedded by a common interest. We, as Québecers, should downplay the fact that "the others" all speak English: language is not the basis of unification among other Canadians as it is among Québecers. We can trace a parallel with the Common Market. No member-country of the Common Market sees "the other countries" as an entity in itself, as homogeneous whole. The fact that they do not have the same language does not allow this perception. Québecois ought to view English Canada from the same perspective.

The model of Canada as a partnership of two peoples or nations is natural for Québec. "Us" and "them." But the other regions of Canada generally have a tendency to see a country more diversified, constructed around several entities, of which one is Québec. In taking account of these different perspectives, the partnership between "us" and the other regions of Canada can be reconciled. This reconciliation will not be a partnership of two, because "they" are more than a single entity. Based on a more solid reality, such a country will represent a more solid partnership.

23

The Canada of Tomorrow

David Johnston: *With this lengthy analysis of Québec and this recognition of a more complex rest of Canada, how do you see Canada of tomorrow?*

Marcel Côté: The existence of the Québec separatist movement, the crisis in public finances, the chronic dependence of the Atlantic provinces on the financial assistance of the federal government, and the growing alienation of the western provinces are equally signs of the serious crisis of Canadian federalism. Profound changes impose themselves. But the setbacks of the last years indicate at what point it is difficult for us to heal the patient. In bringing our discussion to an end, it is useful to sketch out some principles that could guide us, as Québecers (and Québécois), in a reform of Canadian federalism. Canada is a compromise between different regions and different "people" who have certain interests in common. The reform of the Canadian federal system will also be a compromise. Each region approaches the central government with a particular vision. Québec must redefine its vision of Canada.

Obviously this short chapter cannot do justice to the complexity of the challenge represented by a reform of the Canadian constitutional structure. Nevertheless, the broad lines must be traced. Québecers will not be satisfied with the status quo. Although the referendum debate does not bear on the reform of federalism, the promise of reform is essential to a victory by the Canadian side.

Can you spell out the elements of this vision?

First, let me speak as a Québécois, a French-speaking Québecer. Here are some principles that could define a Québécois vision of Canada. The first principle consists in recognizing our identity, as a people, defined essentially by a language, French, and by a territory, Québec. Collectively we also feel that we are "masters of our political destiny" and, indeed, could choose the structures of the country that we want. The Québécois political voice will always be expressed principally and primarily by the government of Québec, the government Québecers control.

Québécois must also recognize an historic responsibility towards the francophone minority elsewhere in Canada, who nonetheless have their own identity and the right to choose a destiny different from ours. We must also recognize a responsibility towards those who define themselves as other than Québécois, and who share with us the territory of Québec. The aboriginal nations have claims as worthwhile if not more so than Québécois in large parts of this territory. Fortunately, as much by their tradition as by right, the aboriginals have agreed to share this territory.

At the same time, nearly a million anglophones who call themselves Canadians first share our territory. Their historic rights are inalienable. We have recognized them for generations, as much because of respect for their rights as for reasons of cooperation in the same economic and social framework. Francophone Québecers must fully accept this important linguistic minority. We should recognize their right to develop in their own language, in a context in which French remains the common language of Québec.

The principles enunciated above are generally shared by Québécois federalists and even by the separatists. But we part around Québec's relations with Canada, and more particularly around the revision of the framework that defines them. For the federalist Québécois are also Canadians. And they want to bring reforms to Canada, not destroy it.

So how does one generate a continuous constructive reform process that could be an alternative to separation?

Just as Québec separatists cannot lead the rest of Canada to negotiate the terms of a separation, so Québécois federalists cannot envisage a fundamental reorganization of Canadian federalism via the mechanisms currently in place to amend the constitution. The two setbacks of Meech and Charlottetown are instructive. It serves no purpose to bring around the negotiation table the eleven Canadian first ministers and the leaders of the territories and the aboriginal nations to formally amend the constitution. The multiplicity of conflicting agendas condemns such an effort to failure.

Rather, Canadians should envisage a continuous process of reform, an evolution of Canadian federalism sensitive, among other things, to the interests of all regions, including Québec. This evolution should not take place principally by way of formal amendments to the constitution. Ententes from government to government could give just as concrete results. The Québec-Canada entente on immigration, in place for seventeen years, illustrates well this method. From time to time a constitutional amendment of limited scope could come to crystallize a consensus. But in general fashion the reorganization of the structures of governance in Canada ought to take place outside the amendment mechanisms set out in the constitution. Québec has nothing to fear from such a process. It is a matter of seeking progress by a series of steps rather than by giant leaps, like the rejected Charlottetown entente or the project of the "beige book" of the Liberal party of Québec in 1980. Experience suggests small steady steps of continuous progress, even if they appear unspectacular when considered in isolation.

The success of such an enterprise depends greatly on the coherence and the continuity of the constitutional positions of Québec. Has this been the case?
The answer is no. The federalists in Québec do not have a coherent vision of what they want. They must define a transparent Canadian project, which clearly situates the place of Québec in Canada, and the longterm objectives that Québec sees in the evolution of the Canadian federal regime.

Can you explain that in more detail?
The constitutional position of the Québécois federalists has vacillated over time. For example, the Allaire Report adopted by the Québec Liberal party in 1992 marked an important break in continuity,

proposing a massive repatriation of the powers held by the federal government. First, Québec should make up its mind between two possible regimes, either the *federal regime,* which we know now, with a federal parliament holding a taxation power, or a *confederal regime,* modeled after the European Common Market, where the major decisions would be taken by a council of representatives of the provinces. The Allaire Report indicated its preference for the latter model. Federal regimes are much more frequent across the world than confederal. Nevertheless, the replacement of the Canadian federal regime with a European type of superstructure has been evoked from time to time in Québec and in western Canada.

In your view is there a "better" regime?

The essence of the Canadian system is the presence in Ottawa of a government that can levy taxes and spend them in its fields of jurisdiction. Over the years this system has led to the development of Canadian fiscal federalism, this immense apparatus of redistributing national revenue between rich and poor regions.

As discussed, Québec is actually a beneficiary of this regime of redistribution. It has not always been thus. It will not always be thus. Regional fortunes change like the seasons. For example, Alberta now contributes more to the system than it takes. Until World War II it was a beneficiary. Québec could also become a net contributor. But beyond these accounting measures there is also an element of stability when recessions strike. Regions most affected by recession temporarily receive aid from the system. Mighty Ontario so benefitted during the last recession. Québec has also benefitted in earlier recessions. These automatic stabilizers are one of the great contributions of Canadian federalism.

While many of the other great functions of the federal government can be realized in a confederal structure, the fiscal redistribution regime can only function in a realistic fashion in a federal regime. The common market system clearly demonstrates the redistribution limits of a confederal regime.

And this leads to a second principle?

Yes. Québec ought to opt clearly for the maintenance of a federal regime, with a Canadian parliament sovereign in matters of taxes and possessing its own competencies, by contrast to a confederal regime.

Such a position implies the maintenance of Québec as one among ten provinces. It also carries with it the necessity of defining the fields of competence of Ottawa and the provinces and the mechanisms to arbitrate the conflicts between the two levels of government.

How could this be done?

All federations must deal with conflicts of jurisdiction between the two levels of government. These conflicts arise from the very nature of the political system. Politicians are invited to address the problems of society. This generally produces clashes between jurisdictional fields. An unemployed person is not preoccupied with constitutional prerogatives of governments: what he or she wants is a job. Politicians are thus led to enlarge the frontiers of their fields of jurisdiction.

The most efficient way to limit these conflicts is to establish the superiority of one of the two levels of government, accompanied by mechanisms of disallowance when the subordinate level goes beyond its limit. Federal regimes in place all have, to varying degrees, such mechanisms. Sometimes they favour the federal level, as in the

United States, sometimes the provincial level, as in Germany. The Canadian federal regime suffers from the clear absence of such mechanisms. This not only feeds frequent conflict but favours a stiff competition between the two levels of government, one of the great causes of our current fiscal crisis.

The advantage of these mechanisms of control is easy to demonstrate. From such mechanisms the municipal authority in Canada is actually subjected to the provincial authority. One speaks rarely of overlaps between these two levels of government. Why? Because provincial governments have the means to disallow municipal governments when they exceed their jurisdictions.

Federal politicians vehemently oppose all efforts to submit the federal level to the discipline of the provincial level. I see them predicting the end of Canada. Politicians unite under the same banner: they want the least limit possible on their powers and employ eloquent arguments to justify their extension. But the people must decide. As the tutelage of provincial governments, and in particular the governments of provinces such as Québec, by the government of Canada is impossible to imagine for historic and sociological reasons, it is the reverse that we ought to envisage.

And this is another basic principle?

Yes. One constant of the constitutional program not only of Québécois but of all reform-minded federalists must be to put in place mechanisms of disavowal of the federal level by the provincial level when the former exceeds its jurisdiction.

Germany is a country united, strong, and efficient. The federal government there is subordinate to the tutelage of the member states, via the German senate, of which the members are representatives named by the states. The term of senators is the same as those elected in the lower chamber. The senate cannot vote out the federal government, but it can disallow or amend all federal laws. The representatives of the states in the senate keep the federal level in its court. The mechanism is simple and highly effective.

Would a similar reform of our senate be sufficient to constrain the federal level and eliminate the inter-level competition and duplications?

The German example suggests yes. This leads one to emphasize that for Canada the answer would be "probably yes," although only time and trial and error would tell.

The most important thing is that such a reform, because of its limited scope, is possible in Canada. Provincial leaders and federal politicians, tired of all those years of bickering, could form a strategic alliance with a view to such a simple reform, focusing on the nomination of senators and the duration of their mandate.

It is important to keep the proposition simple. For instance, a senate reform proposal was found in the 1980 beige book of the Liberal party of Québec. But the proposal was then accompanied by a plethora of propositions on other subjects, making of the beige book a much too ambitious project with no chance of being adopted. It never was. Reforming the senate would require a constitutional amendment and unanimity. Can one obtain it without unleashing a pack of additional revindications? That's not certain. But it has the merit of being limited in scope, which makes it more plausible. It is also supported by the German experience, which is powerful.

What about a clearer distinction in the fields of competence?
A new sharing of responsibilities and jurisdictions between governments could also simplify the functioning of Canadian federalism, and cut down on the frequency of the sterile quarrels of jurisdiction. But a constitutional amendment on the fields of jurisdiction is scarcely plausible. We will never reach agreement. Sectoral ententes, government to government, of limited scope, can be just as effective. The Québec-Canada immigration entente, negotiated, let us repeat, between the Trudeau and Lévesque governments, is a model. It could be repeated for manpower training, the object of quarrels for many years. Indeed, two or three ententes of this type could be sufficient to assure constitutional peace between Ottawa and Québec for several decades.

It is not that our politicians do not want reorganizations of greater sweep. But they have conflicting agendas. Thus, one must be wary of the pretensions of politicians, whether provincial or federal, in these jurisdictional battles. Both sides are guilty of abuse. A massive realignment of responsibilities is neither necessary nor necessarily welcome. In a field as sensitive as culture, Québecers perhaps have more reasons to distrust the inexperience of Québec's ministers of cultural affairs than the federal cultural institutions such as the Canada Council and CBC. These institutions have served Québec culture well, although normally culture should belong only to Québec. To blame Ottawa is often a manner by which provincial politicians exculpate themselves for their own failings.

Can one not imagine more success in harmonization and reciprocity of powers and programs?

Yes. One should imagine an evolution over time towards better federal-provincial cooperation in fields of competence. In the next few years, the federal and provincial governments will have to cope with the debt crisis: they will be urgently summoned to re-examine their social programs, to eliminate inefficiencies, and to relieve public finances. We are spending well beyond our wealth base. This will be an occasion to eliminate from federal laws the principle of national standards, a means used by the federal level to impose a rigid cost structure in many social programs.

National standards give to Ottawa the mandate to fix the minimum criteria of services for programs managed by the provinces. One finds them, among others, in health and in social programs, and in subsidized housing. The federal government justifies their imposition as the condition of its financial participation. "I finance, therefore I establish the base conditions." This policy has some very unfortunate consequences, because it discourages experimentation and adaptation to local conditions.

Does this lead to another principle?

Yes. The policy of national standards ought to be gradually replaced by the principle of reciprocal treatment for the citizens. A citizen of province A who uses a program of province B should not suffer discrimination and should be treated as all other citizens of province B. The application of this principle favours a harmonization of the programs from one province to the other while respecting local particularities. One already finds this reciprocity and harmonization operating in various programs such as the Québec and Canada pension plans. But the principle ought to be pushed much further. For example, the students from Newfoundland at any university in another province ought to pay the same tuition fees as students from those provinces.

They do at present.
There will be pressure to change this, because provinces will see painless extra revenues in extra fees for out-of-province students. Thus, the policy of national standards ought to be replaced by the principle of reciprocal treatment of citizens for programs of a national character belonging to the provinces.

This change could gradually facilitate the search for innovative solutions to the financial crisis that endangers the survival of our social programs and the social security net of which we are so proud and which makes us the envy of the entire world. Canadians will not be worse off.

What about Québécois' expectations of Canadians?
Québécois ought to accept Canada for what it is, our country. This is not to say that we are no longer Québécois, and we do not diminish our reality as a people who are masters of our destiny. But if we decide to live in Canada, we must also accept this reality. One can at the same time be a Québécois and a Canadian. As a federation, Canada recognizes this "double belonging." As the Québécois people, our first government is that of the province of Québec. But the government of Canada is also our government and Canada is our country. In it we have some partners. It is the best country in the world, if one accepts the judgement of non-Canadians.

Thus we can be proud of being Canadians, just as we are proud to be Québécois. This pride will help us to play the Canadian card, a card essential to our collective development. Canada remains for Québec the economic and political framework, *par excellence*. Just as well to use it.

In putting aside their traditional ambivalence towards their attachment to Canada, Québécois will be able to make better allies elsewhere in Canada and to influence, in the context of their best interests, the evolution of the Canadian political structures.

24

The Good Choice

David Johnston: *Given this refreshing appraisal of Québec in Canada, how do you appraise the choice soon to be made by Québecers?*

Marcel Côté: We shall soon be called to choose the country that we want for tomorrow. On the one side is the country that we know, Québec in Canada, a reality that is familiar to us. It has advantages and disadvantages. Its principal advantage is that it is known.

On the other side is a promised land. According to the prophets of this option, this land will be infinitely superior to the country we actually have. Liberated from the domination of the rest of Canada, which according to the indépendantistes brakes us now, we shall perform miracles as a people. But is this rather the illusion of sweet-talkers? If our government were so good, there would not be a crisis in education, in the construction sector, and so on.

But whatever this promised land might be, it is not at our door for the moment. It is necessary first to arrive. The Québec people must cross a desert before getting there. The costs of this long march to the promised land can be assessed.

These are the costs that we have tried to describe in this extended conversation. What happens to milk farmers; in Hull-Gatineau; in Montréal. These are the principal shocks. But they are of an amplitude to have profound repercussions throughout Québec. The promoters of independence will deny the reality of these shocks. Yes, English Canada will continue to buy our milk, at twice the world price. Yes, we shall create thousands of jobs for civil servants in Hull. No, the English will not leave Montréal, because we will treat them well. To present these illusions as reality is the most cruel discourse that one can inflict on those who trust us.

We have also tried to show that to add the federal budgetary malady to that of Québec's, while eliminating the net benefits that we receive from the regime, and factoring in the effect of a recession, will create an even bigger financial malady. No, Québec could not sell an unlimited amount of debt abroad. It would be necessary to cut. Not $1-billion, not $3-billion, not $5-billion. Much more. Ten billion dollars and perhaps much more. And in less than a year. This is impossible. This is why a sensible government would not launch us into this adventure.

Separatist politicians invoke the savings resulting from the elimination of duplications to say that "this will not go badly." It is so easy to exaggerate the savings from the elimination of federal-provincial duplication. Will anyone do a serious accounting analysis of these duplications, to identify them with precision? This exercise has never been done.

We have tried to demonstrate the fragility of an entente between Canada and Québec on common currency. The exercise might have seemed complex and difficult to understand to some, with too many figures. But thus it is with finances, and particularly international finances. Québecers should not allow themselves to be lulled to sleep with seventy-five-year-old examples of shared currency in preindustrial economies! We live in a different financial and monetary reality, which merits more respect and caution. There now exist "rules of convergence" that allow us to determine if a common currency can be shared in an economy as advanced as ours. Québec does not meet the rules. People moving their savings out of this artificial currency zone would precipitate a liquidity crisis. Recall the two key factors leading to a crisis: a government as indebted as the Québec government would be and households that have $75-billion in liquid savings and want to protect their value.

Finally, remember that the crisis can happen without warning, as was the case in Sweden. When it does happen, the government will try to deny its existence. "Don't panic," it will say. That is its role. But examples elsewhere are also valid for Québec. Those who listen to the government will be the big losers.

Our would-be marathoners Paul and Virginia are fictitious persons. But to say to someone who thinks of running the marathon, "Get in shape," is not an act of terrorism. It is an act of intelligence and care. Those who launch accusations of terrorism have the right to freedom of speech, but they do not in this way enrich the political debate in Québec, on that which is surely the most important and most critical subject for us all as a people.

What then is the destiny of Québecers?

The choice that we confront this year is not new. The people of Québec have always had to adjust to an everyday reality, which is far from an ideal world. History has seen us develop as a society in the political whole that is Canada. The consequences of this infuse our reality every day. It is not only the presence here of nearly one million Québec anglophones, nor the fact of the integration of our economy in the Canadian whole. It is also our everyday life, the currency that we use, the passport, telephone rates, markets for our products, equilibrium in our public finances. A thousand and one hooks attach Québecers to a Canadian reality.

Canada is not an ideal country. No country is. But we ought to accept its reality, its complexity, weaknesses in its federal regime, its problems in its public finances. We must not play ostrich. This reality is also ours, as Québecers.

Does there exist a terrestrial paradise where the world is ordered just as we would like? Evidently not. Even the indépendantistes don't believe that. But they support, nevertheless, a decoupling of Canada, believing that in reorganizing among ourselves we will have a better world in which the problems are suddenly easier to regulate.

The promised land exists only in dreams. In everyday life, one must accept an imperfect reality, full of constraints, a world where no people is truly independent. To change the political regime is not in itself impossible. But such a change will not make reality disappear. To change that regime is very costly. As always, the less fortunate, the weakest, the most vulnerable will pay the bill.

The choice for Canada is a much superior choice.